Make Sense

Make Sense

Creative and **critical** thinking

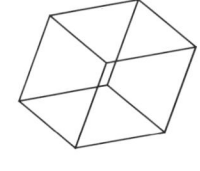

imagination

Sandy Cahir

Nelson

logic

Thomas Nelson & Sons Ltd
Nelson House
Mayfield Road
Walton-on-Thames
Surrey KT12 5PL
United Kingdom

I(T)P® Thomas Nelson is an International
    Thomson Publishing Company
I(T)P® is used under licence

© Sandy Cahir 1995

First published in the UK by Thomas Nelson & Sons Ltd 1997
ISBN 0-17-432586-X
NPN 9 8 7 6 5 4 3 2 1
01 00 99 98 97

All rights reserved. No part of this publication may be reproduced,
copied or transmitted in any form or by any means, electronic or
mechanical, including photocopy, recording, or any information
storage and retrieval system, without permission in writing from
the publisher or under licence from the Copyright Licensing
Authority Ltd, 90 Tottenham Court Road, London W1P 9HE.

Typeset by Syarikat Seng Teik Sdn. Bhd., Malaysia

Printed and bound in Malaysia

Contents

Introduction		vii

PART ONE Thinking Critically

1	SHARPEN YOUR WITS	Testing Powers of Logic	3
2	HOW DO YOU KNOW THAT?	Facts and Opinions	8
3	SPEAKING GENERALLY	Generalisations and Evidence	14
4	AUDIENCE AND PURPOSE:	Who Are They? What Is It?	23
5	I CONTEND THAT . . .	Establishing a Viewpoint	27
6	DESIGNING PERSUASIVE PARAGRAPHS	Essentials of a Good Paragraph	33
7	SKILFUL SUMMARIES	Effective Summary Techniques	40
8	EVERY EFFECT HAS A CAUSE	Understanding their Relationship	46
9	JUST LETTING YOU KNOW	Writing Informatively	55
10	THOUGHTS ON PAPER	Argumentative Writing	63

PART TWO Thinking Creatively

11	RELATIVELY SPEAKING	Constructing Analogies	77
12	THE ART OF BRAINSTORMING	Creative Planning	82
13	THE IMAGE BEFORE US	Cartoons and Photographs	86
14	I SAY THIS, YOU SAY THAT	Comparing Attitudes Through Songs	93
15	THINKING CREATIVELY	A Pathway to Effective Thinking	99
16	GENTLE PERSUASION	Language of Influence	103
17	'THE LEARNED OPPOSITION IS . . .'	Debating Techniques	113
18	ISSUES IN FILM	*The Emerald Forest*	120
19	PROBLEM SOLVING	Creative Critical Thinking	127

PART THREE   On Assignment

20 HUMAN RIGHTS — 135
21 ABORIGINES AND AUSTRALIA — 146
22 UNDERSTANDING DISABILITY — 155

Appendix 1   The Language of Thinking — 163
Bibliography — 164
Further Reading — 165
Acknowledgments — 166
Index — 167

Introduction

Make Sense is a course of study aimed at helping Year 9 and 10 students understand the finer points of exploring issues. It is designed as a transition course to the study of issues in Years 11 and 12.

It highlights some of those areas that need more attention in senior years, but for which time is a problem. One of these is audience and purpose. Some others include structuring an argument, writing informatively, analysing words and images, and developing contentions. Appendix 1 provides a list of the key terms used in creative and critical thinking.

The course takes students through a range of structured tasks, leading to more complex analyses of resource material. The intention has been to focus both on the logical/critical processes of thought and on the creative functions of thought that are becoming part of daily life. Students are introduced to the features and processes of problem solving, which can be applied outside the English classroom. Some of Edward de Bono's principles on lateral thought have provided a basis for a number of the exercises and approaches.

The range of tasks, and the material available, will help students learn new skills and understand how they, individually, learn best. *Make Sense* also relates to the levels, strands and texts of the National Curriculum.

Sandy Cahir

Part One

Thinking critically

1

Sharpen your wits

Testing powers of logic

Everyone knows that logic is the basis of good thinking. But is it?

Edward de Bono

Thinking can be fun. Sharpen your wits on the following mind-benders, some of which have been adapted from Arthur Mee, *The Children's Encyclopedia* and H.J. Eysenck, *Know Your Own IQ*. Some of them require you to see how one idea connects to another, some to think a little differently from usual, some test your knowledge, and some cause you to think about your powers of observation. All will enable you to understand your own skills and to see how quickly and accurately you think. (The answers are at the end of the chapter.)

Time to think

1 If the dog sat on the tucker box 'five miles from Gundagai' and you left Gundagai at precisely midday, travelling towards the dog at 60 miles per hour, at what time would you pass the dog?

2 The following words have been jumbled. Unjumble them and underline the one that is not a make of car.
ISMHTSIUBI   RJAUGA
DINHYUA   SNAISN
HISSU

3 Underline the odd-one-out.
POSSUM   KANGAROO   WOMBAT   KOALA   WALLABY

4 Underline the jumbled word that is not an Australian poet.
STEAK   SWNALO
TGWIHR   NEISDN
PHOE

5 In Greek mythology, Oedipus, son of Laius and Jocasta, was adopted by Polybus, King of Corinth. Oedipus killed Laius and married Jocasta. They had four

children: Eteocles, Polyneices, Ismene, and Antigone. What relationship does each of the following have to the four children?
Laius
Polybus
Jocasta

6 Complete this sequence.
C E I O __

7 Insert the missing word.
Old is to new as hot is to ____

8 A farmer had a broody hen, but no rooster. The hen would not move off the nest. In order not to let this opportunity pass by, the farmer bought six one-day-old chicks and put them under the hen. The hen immediately moved off the nest, convinced that the chicks were her own. How many eggs had she laid?

9 Two sheep were standing in a paddock, one facing due north and the other facing due south. How could each see the other without turning around?

10 The three letters in the brackets make a word by themselves, but they are also part of two other words. The first word begins with H and ends with the third letter in the brackets. The second word starts with the first letter in the brackets and ends with EN. Insert the word that completes the first word and starts the second.
H(. . .)EN

11 Insert three letters in the brackets that, when prefixed by any of the letters on the left, form a new word.
ST
L
B   (. . .)
AL
Z
PH

12 To each of these words add the prefix that reverses its meaning.
contented   proper   visible   pleasant   ingenuous   natural

13 To which of these Greek adjectives is an 's' added to make the name of a science?
logic   dynamic   optic   metaphysic   rhetoric   physic   politic

14 A frog fell down a well that was 30 metres deep. It climbed up three metres every day and slipped back two metres every night. How long did it take the frog to reach the top?

15 A man looks at a portrait on a wall and says: 'I have no brothers and sisters, but this man's father is my father's son.' Whose portrait is it?

16 In another three years Ben will be three times as old as he was three years ago. How old is he now?

17 Complete this sequence.
 14   19   25   32   __

18 Which word does not belong?
CARROT   ONION   TOMATO   CABBAGE   ZUCCHINI

19 To prepare for a trip to Katmandu, two girls went for a walking tour in the Snowy Mountains. For the total seven days the average distance they walked per day was 15 kilometres. The average for the first four days was 18 kilometres per day. What was the average for the other three days of the tour?

20 What is wrong with these sentences?
In the early 1900s the fear of tuberculosis caused the periodic closure of some schools. The books of the students and the teachers of the schools were ordered to be destroyed.

Answers

1 12.05 p.m.

2 Sushi (Mitsubishi, Hyundai, Jaguar and Nissan are all makes of car. Sushi is a Japanese food.)

3 Koala (The others are marsupials with tails.)

4 Keats is English. The Australian poets are Wright, Hope, Lawson and Dennis.

5 Laius — Grandfather
Polybus — Adoptive Grandfather
Jocasta — Mother and Grandmother

6 W (E is the second letter after C, I is the fourth letter after E, O is the sixth letter after I, and W is the eighth letter after I.)

7 Cold (They are opposites.)

8 None

9 As they stood, they could see each other, one facing north and the other facing south.

10 Old

11 One

12 discontented, improper, invisible, unpleasant, disingenuous, unnatural

13 Physics

14 The first day the frog reached a height of 3 metres, before slipping back to 1 metre. On the second, it reached 4 metres, before falling back to 2 metres. Thus, on the 27th day it reached 29 metres, before slipping back to 27 metres, and on the 28th day it reached 30 metres, but as it was at the top it did not slip back again. Therefore the frog took 28 days to climb to the top.

15 The man says he has no brothers and sisters, therefore his father has only one son — himself. Expressed simply, he says, 'This man's father is myself'. This means that the portrait was of his own son.

16 In another three years Ben will be six years older than he was three years ago. If his age is then three times what it was three years ago, six years must be twice his age three years ago. So he was three years old three years ago, and he is six years old now.

17 40 (The numbers increase by 5, then 6, then 7, and finally by 8.)

18 Tomato (It is a fruit, the others are vegetables.)

19 If the average for seven days was 15 kilometres, the total number of kilometres walked in the seven days must have been 105. If the average for the first four days was 18, the kilometres walked in the first four days must have been 72. Thus there must have been 33 kilometres walked in the last three days, an average of 11 kilometres per day.

20 The second sentence is faulty. It needs to be rewritten to make it clear that it is only the books (and not the teachers) that are to be destroyed.

★ **Thinking critically requires skill and confidence.**

★ **Thinking is a complex process that involves consideration of facts, questioning of evidence and assumptions, use of prior knowledge, and reliance on memory.**

2

How do you know that?

Facts and opinions

You cannot ask us to take sides against the obvious facts of the situation.

Winston Churchill

Writers and public speakers use language to convince their audience, and their attempts to emphasise an opinion or argument are often extremely persuasive. On closer examination, however, there is sometimes something missing. This missing 'something' is often factual detail. To be convincing, an opinion must be supported by fact, regardless of the expertise of the person expressing it.

What's the difference?

A fact is something that *has* been established as true. An opinion is an expression of a view or belief, which *has not* been established as true.

Time to think

1 The following statements are either facts or opinions. Read them and decide which is which.
- Girls are stronger than boys.
- 'With increased illiteracy, the video culture may be contributing to rising violence.' (*Age*, 22 September 1993)
- Years after the death of a star we can still see its light.
- 'I think video games are tough on kids.' (*Australian Educator* No.1, Winter 1993)
- A dog is a quadruped.
- 'On 14 December 1993 Toyota stood down 800 workers at its Dandenong plant.' (*Age*, 15 December 1993)
- Violence on television is desensitising our younger generation.
- All students enjoy studying.
- Not all sharks will attack a human being.
- In Shakespeare's play *Romeo and Juliet*, Juliet kills herself with Romeo's dagger.
- The inner ear contains five chambers filled with fluid — the three semicircular canals, the sacculus and the intriculus.
- The number of whales seen in Australian waters is increasing.

Questioning the facts — supporting the opinions

In the above exercise you may have had some difficulty with the last three statements. While you might have thought that each was a fact, you may have felt the need for more information — more evidence. For example, the third last requires a quick reference to the final section of the play, or to a teacher who knows the play; the second last, although it sounds believable, requires a reference to a medical text; and the last requires some statistical evidence before it could be accepted as a fact, rather than an opinion.

You may think that a particular statement is factual because it sounds true, but a person presenting a certain point of view often relies on this lack of information to make the argument sound convincing. You may have heard statements such as: 'Don't confuse the issue with facts', or 'Facts ruin good arguments'. It is human nature to want to be persuasive in expressing a viewpoint, without necessarily having evidence to support it.

Time to think

1 What information or factual detail is necessary before the following statements can be accepted? Discuss your responses in groups.
- It is a fact that when a person is lying to you, he or she won't look you in the eye.
- Australia is the world's largest island.
- English is a compulsory subject in all States of Australia.
- The blue colour of the sky is caused by sunlight reflecting off dust particles in space.
- Kangaroos are descended from giant kangaroos from the Jurassic era.
- The *Argus* was Melbourne's first daily newspaper.
- At any point in world history, there has been conflict of some sort, of some size, in some place.
- Immigration to Australia is increasing.
- The number of students wishing to obtain tertiary qualifications is higher now than it was ten years ago.
- Medical science is researching the possibility of men bearing babies.

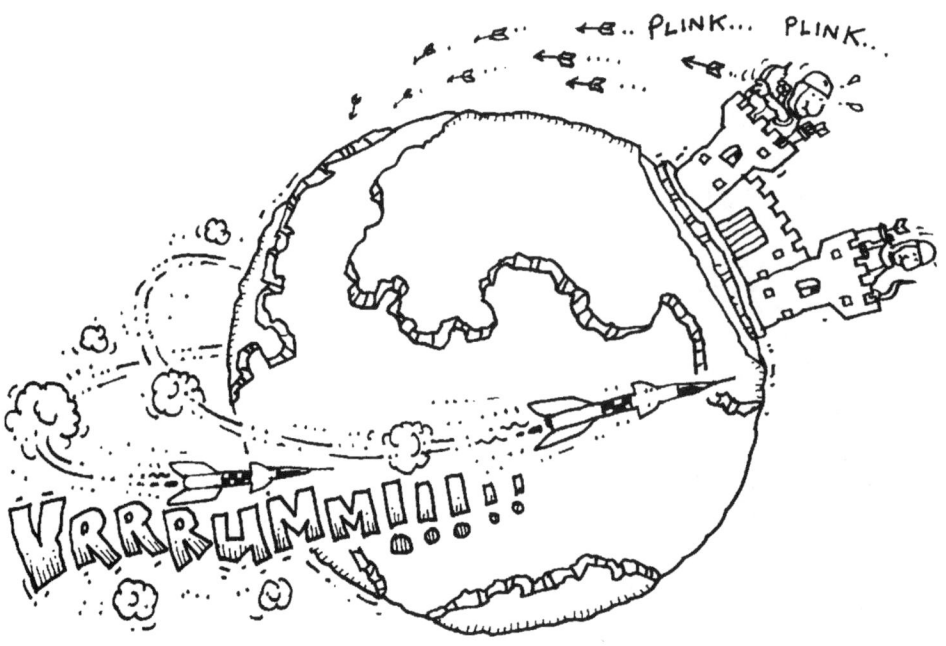

Expressing an opinion

Different people throughout the world have different opinions, but whether or not their opinions are based upon fact is open to discussion. Sometimes supporting facts are not easily available. Here are some different views on how the earth and human beings came into existence.

> In the creation account of the Ngadju Dyak, the clouds, hills, sun and moon, etc., are created by the 'clashing' of two mountains. The first man and woman are made out of the debris resulting from a battle between two hornbills . . . in the Tree of Life, which is destroyed in the process.
>
> **(Maclagan,** *Creation Myths: Man's Introduction to the World***)**

> Evolution is the process by which present-day animal species originated from more simple forms. The changes occurred by degrees and over many millennia, going from a few simple species to many complex ones. [The evolution theory has as its basis the idea that a dense mass in space exploded with a Big Bang, hurling pieces out to form the planets as we know them today.]
>
> **(***The Macquarie History of Ideas***)**

> Over a period of six days, God created heaven and earth, night and day, all geographical forms, all animal and plant life, and on the seventh day God rested.
>
> **(Biblical view of creation)**

> [T]he uncreated and eternal earth had always existed as a large flat disc floating in space. Its uninhabited surface was a vast featureless plain, extending unbroken to the horizon. No hills or watercourses broke its monotonous surface, no trees or grass covered its nakedness, nor did the calls of birds or animals disturb its quiet. It was a dead world. Yet, slumbering beneath that monotonous surface, were indeterminate forms of life that would eventually transform it into the world which the aborigines know today.
>
> **(Roberts and Mountford,** *The Dreamtime Book: Australian Aboriginal Myths***)**

Time to think

1 Having read the four views above, discuss each one with a partner.
- Which are likely to be supported by facts?
- What is your view on the origins of humankind?
- What facts support your view?

2 In this chapter you have read and commented upon the facts and opinions presented by others. Now test yourself. Make a list of five facts and another of five opinions. Choose any subjects that are of interest to you. How definitely can you state that a fact is a fact? Can you support your five opinions with facts?

Identifying facts and opinions

While you can justifiably be sceptical about an opinion, it is harder to judge whether or not facts presented as evidence should be believed.

Time to think

1 The article 'Gender Roles Still Entrenched' by Sue Neales (*Age*, 16 December 1993) combines fact and opinion. Read it then draw up two columns, one headed 'Facts', the other headed 'Opinions', and list the facts and opinions in the appropriate columns. Don't forget the headline. Compare your findings with a partner.

Gender roles still entrenched

Sally and Tom Alvin are not your typical couple. They don't watch much television, they both play sport for hours each day and Carlton footballer Tom holds down two jobs while still cooking the odd meal.

Most unusual of all, Sally thinks Tom probably spends more of his day talking than she does.

According to the latest Australian Bureau of Statistics 1992 household time-use study released yesterday, these habits make the Alvin family something of a rarity.

The report, 'How Australians use their time', found that gender roles in society were still well and truly entrenched.

While men and women spent equal amounts of time working – an average of seven hours a day – women still devote more hours to housework.

The cooking, cleaning, laundry and child-care duties are still largely borne by women, while men remain kings of the garden, garage, and dustbins.

And while men spend 64 per cent of their time nominated as 'working' in the paid workforce, unpaid labor, mainly household work, accounted for 70 per cent of total work for women.

In total, the study found that Australians spent 49 million hours every day on household chores last year and 44 million hours on paid labor.

But the ABS figures also provide an insight into the way Australians spend their time when they are not conventionally working.

Among other features it showed that women spend a total of two hours and 21 minutes talking each day to family friends and on the phone, while men converse for less than two hours; country people are more community conscious and friendly than their city counterparts; the average time spent sleeping is eight hours and 20 minutes a day.

Men, on average, spend 21 minutes a day fixing the house and the car, while women spend 76 minutes a day preparing meals and cleaning up, 36 minutes a day doing the laundry and 44 minutes in other household jobs.

- ★ A fact is something that has been established as true.
- ★ An opinion is the expression of a particular view or belief, which has not been established as true.
- ★ To be convincing, an opinion must be supported by fact.
- ★ Evidence can help you to tell the difference between statements of fact and statements of opinion.

3

Speaking generally

Generalisations and evidence

*'O dull, one-sided voice,' said I,
Wilt thou make everything a lie,'*

Tennyson, *The Two Voices*

What happens when you don't think carefully before you speak and you don't have supporting information?

Sometimes a simple discussion with another person can change into a heated disagreement. For example, when one or the other person feels he or she is running out of factual details to support an opinion, other, more desperate, attempts at persuasion can occur, particularly if a battle of wills becomes the driving force behind the disagreement. These attempts could include the use of generalisation to emphasise a point. For example, parents discussing the choice of a particular school for their children might end up arguing. The father might make a comment about the school having good sporting facilities, to which the mother might reply, 'That's typical of males, always thinking of sporting facilities.' The mother has become angry with one male in particular, and has made a generalisation about all males.

Identifying generalisations

A generalisation is a statement made about a whole group. Sometimes the statement will be accurate, but at other times the evidence will be too limited to be true about all individuals within that group. It is often a mistake to make a comment about a whole group based on what you know about one individual within it, but the desire to win an argument often causes people to make statements that they know are untrue. For example, an angry parent, losing a battle with a child playing computer games, might exclaim, 'All computer games are mindless'. Although the parent may be fully aware that some computer games are educational, anger has caused the parent to make an inaccurate judgement or generalisation about *all* computer games.

Time to think

1 Each of the statements below makes an observation about a particular group and includes a generalisation. Read each carefully and complete the tasks that follow:

> **From this class it's clear that girls will always be better organised than boys.**
> **Obviously people who play football enjoy rough sports.**
> **Wind instruments are difficult to play.**
> **All fifteen-year-old boys are good chefs.**
> **Old horses are no good for riding.**
> **Dreams always tell the future.**
> **All teenage boys love throwing rubbish into bins in classrooms.**
> **Adolescents are becoming illiterate as a result of computer games.**

> **English teachers enjoy teaching Shakespeare.**
> **Sport commentators cannot speak properly.**

- Name the group involved in each generalisation.
- Identify the generalisation being made.
- State why the generalisation is not accurate.

The language of generalisation

It is important to structure your sentences in English carefully so that you express yourself clearly. What might appear to be a simple misuse of a word can completely change the intended meaning.

For example, the following sentence can be altered by using different language to create different meanings.

> **Students enjoy thinking.**

This is an obvious generalisation to which the following changes can be made:

> **All students enjoy thinking.**
> **Some students enjoy thinking.**
> **Students enjoy thinking occasionally.**
> **Not many students enjoy thinking.**
> **A majority of students enjoy thinking.**
> **Sometimes students enjoy thinking.**
> **A few students enjoy thinking.**
> **Many students enjoy thinking.**

The process of altering the language is known as modifying or qualifying. Using this process can turn an unacceptable statement into an acceptable one.

Time to think

1 Here are some words and phrases that can be used to modify statements.

some	not many
most	a majority
can be	in some instances
a few	a significant number
many	a minority
all	a proportion of
rarely	almost all

Add four of your own to the list.

2 Modify the six sentences below using words and phrases from your own list and the list provided. Try to create accuracy in the point of view being expressed. If you have trouble you might need to change the structure of the sentences. Play around with the language until you feel it is right.
- Education is for vocational training.
- Uncovering the identity of biological mothers in adoption cases always leads to unexpected and difficult outcomes.
- All alternative therapies currently available are worthwhile.
- Computers are causing illiteracy in adolescents.
- School is boring.
- All our planet's rainforests are being destroyed.

Simple generalisations

A simple generalisation functions at a straightforward level. It is easy to generalise that, for example, 'Lollies are harmful to your teeth'. This is not hard to understand or believe. It is a general statement made about a group. On the basis of prior knowledge of the connection sugar has to tooth decay, the generalisation is acceptable.

Clearly there are circumstances in which generalisations are acceptable. For example, where there is prior knowledge in the audience or where the generalisation serves the purpose of introducing a topic. However, generalisations are not sufficient (and are therefore unacceptable) to support a case.

So, while 'Lollies are harmful to your teeth' is an acceptable generalisation, additional argument would need evidence, such as, 'A recent survey showed that 79 per cent of children who eat lollies had tooth decay, compared with only 38 per cent of those who do not eat lollies.' This use of facts is a better way of supporting a statement than the alternative of using a second generalisation. A second generalisation, such as, 'If you eat lollies you will have a toothache', would be unacceptable as evidence.

Time to think

1 Using the example above as a guide, construct some simple generalisations about the following subjects:
   grandfathers
   chocolate cakes
   giraffes
   homework
   cars

Complex generalisations

More complex generalisations can create controversy, particularly when they express opinions that contain value judgements. A value judgement is a personal observation that reflects your own biases or social attitudes.

All people, for one reason or another, place their own emphasis on certain objects, attitudes or issues. An issue may be so important to an individual or group that it becomes an obsession or a cause. For example, those people who set out in rubber dinghies to obstruct the passage of nuclear-powered ships into Australian ports are expressing their personal views on the use of nuclear energy. They value a nuclear-free environment, and are prepared to risk their lives to demonstrate their point. These people have a bias against nuclear energy, because of its harmful and life-threatening consequences. While they are expressing a clear personal view, they are also reflecting a social attitude. In taking this course of action, they are making a value judgement on the issue of nuclear-powered ships coming into Australian ports.

Here are some guidelines for examining value judgements, which you might find useful.

- What is being 'valued'?
- Who or what is being judged?
- What observations have been made about the group, person or issue concerned?
- Explain the personal bias shown towards the subject.
- State the issue being explored and the attitude expressed.

Time to think

1 Use the guidelines above to analyse each of the statements below.
   - If you don't smoke you're not cool.
   - Euthanasia is wrong.
   - Timber workers don't care for the environment.
   - People who have a lot of money care more about money than about people.
   - People with white skin are not as good at sport as people with black skin.
   - Parents are to blame for the misdeeds of children.

- Experimentation on innocent animals for the benefit of humans is callous and thoughtless and should be banned.
- We learn a lot from the media.
- Real estate agents are an essential part of our society.
- Inadequate care is available for the elderly.

Giving evidence

When you make a general statement that you want others to believe, it is important to provide evidence. For example, if you were arguing that parents should not be concerned about the spread of illnesses in child-care centres, you might support your view with evidence, such as the strict guidelines that child-care centres have about hygiene procedures and the admission of children with infectious diseases.

Time to think

1 Have another look at the value judgements in the exercise above. In order for these statements to be acceptable, they need supporting evidence. What evidence makes each one acceptable?

2 The article below, from *The Gaia Atlas of Planet Management*, which explores the management of forests, shows how important it is to plan the replanting of forests with the future in mind. A number of general statements are made and supported by evidence. Read the article carefully and complete the tasks that follow.

Forests of the future

Planting tomorrow's trees

In the North, we can safely say that we know a good deal about how to manage forests. In the forests of the South, by contrast, we have scarcely made a start. Ironically, much of the problem lies with the streamlined techniques developed in the North. Many mechanized logging operations in the tropics are wasteful and destructive: often 75% of the surrounding canopy is damaged during one operation to extract a few commercially valuable species. Unlike temperate forests, tropical forests are unable to withstand such disruption because of their ecological complexity. In fact, tropical and temperate forests are so dissimilar that it would probably be better if we did not use the same word 'forest' to describe them.

The main advance in the North in recent years has been in genetic engineering. Trees grown from tissue culture can quickly reforest large areas of denuded land. Also, geneticists are learning

(continued)

how to isolate the genes that make a tree species grow straight and tall, or produce wood with high tensile strength – whereupon they can replicate such prize characteristics in identical trees in large numbers.

But in the South, because of the critical role played by tropical forests... it is better to establish 'tree farms' on lands already deforested than to harvest the natural forest. A plantation of eucalyptus or pine can generate ten times as much sustainable harvest as can a patch of virgin forest. But a plantation costs at least $1000 per hectare to establish, let alone to maintain; and the present rate of tree planting is not even one-tenth of the rate at which natural forests are being logged and degraded.

Fuelwood plantations are also urgently required to relieve pressure on natural forests. We need more trees around farms and in village woodlots, at least five times as many in the Third World as a whole right now, and between 20 and 50 times as many in certain African states. The difficulties, however, are not financial. Community forestry relies on the involvement of local people. If everybody's views are sought from the start, hopefully everybody will plant trees and tend them, and everybody will ensure that the harvesting system produces a regular supply of fuelwood.

Similar community efforts are needed to rehabilitate denuded watersheds in the South. In China, South Korea, and parts of India, there has been much success, due to the close coordination of planners and villagers.

Tropical and temperate forests are so different in their biological makeup, that they need two fundamentally different approaches to their management. Temperate forests are actually expanding slightly, due to reforestation in the North. Densely settled zones such as southern West Germany are one-quarter covered with forests... Much land, however, is still under-utilized: Scotland, for example, could accommodate much more tree cover.

Recycling paper

Developed countries could reduce their demand for paperpulp by at least one-quarter, simply through greater recycling. During World War II, most Northern countries recovered as much as half of their paper.

Forest management in the South

In most developing countries, forestry departments are understaffed and underfunded. Foresters see their main duty as keeping people out of forests, rather than helping them to establish woodlots, fuelwood plantations, and other village forestry projects. Fortunately, international agencies such as the World Bank are now taking the preservation of tropical forests seriously, and are promoting forestry as an important aspect of rural development. Although the Bank has no effective system for ensuring that ecological considerations are introduced at the outset of all projects, it can choose to withdraw aid if the project proves to be environmentally unsound. Recently, the Bank withdrew support for a Colombian cattle-ranching project after surveys showed the forest soils to be incapable of supporting large-scale development.

Replanting watersheds

Nations are realizing the value of restoring tree cover on upland watersheds – a measure that benefits virtually everyone in the community. Although implemented on far too limited a scale as yet, this is an encouraging step forward.

Community forestry

Supported by international development agencies, many countries are encouraging their people to become actively involved in establishing fuelwood plantations. In Gujarat, India, schoolchildren may soon be raising as many tree seedlings as the government.

Cloning trees

Douglas firs, American sycamores, and several other species may soon sprout like mushrooms, thanks to recent advances in genetic engineering. They will grow straighter and produce denser wood. Modern forestry should progress even more by the year 2000.

(continued)

> ***The forests of West Germany***
>
> Covering a third of the country, these forests occupy an important place in the national psyche. According to Chancellor Kohl, they are 'of inestimable importance for the water cycle, for our climate, for our health, for our recreation, and for the identity of the German landscape.'
>
> ***A sustainable land-use system***
>
> A strategy with much potential is agro-forestry, which amounts to growing trees and food crops alongside each other. Forest land and marginal land, normally rated unsuitable for crops, can be utilized for the production of food. Certain tree species, notably the leguminous ones, fix atmospheric nitrogen in the soil, thereby helping to rehabilitate degraded forestlands.
>
> ***The Chipko movement***
>
> In 1974, the women of Reni in northern India took simple but effective action to stop tree felling. They threatened to hug the trees if the lumberjacks attempted to fell them. The women's protest (known as the Chipko movement) saved 12 000 sq km of sensitive watershed.

- Identify the generalisations.
- List the supporting evidence following each generalisation.
- What evidence can you find to suggest that people are concerned about trees in their environments?
- Consider the guidelines for examining value judgements given above, and explain what is 'valued' in this article. Does it favour a particular viewpoint? Is it promoting a social attitude?

3 Think about your own environment. What observations can you make about conservation in your area? Have any local forests been destroyed? Are trees of major concern to your local council? Are there many trees in your area? These and many other questions arise when you start thinking about yourself in the environment of the future.

- Make a list of generalisations, and the supporting evidence, that relates to your own local environment.

4 Working in groups, select one of the following situations and create a dramatic presentation. Be sure to think about the generalisations and evidence connected with each.

- You live deep in the bush among some very tall gum trees. One day you wake up to the sound of bulldozers crashing through the bush. To your horror, the bush is alive with the buzz and rattle of saws. You think of the animals within. Explore the possibilities of this scenario.
- Dolphins have always held a special place in your heart, but you have not seen one in the wild until today. Your sighting is destroyed by the tangle of garbage lying along this picturesque coastline. The dolphins' future is at risk. What do you do?
- You live next door to a minimal-disease piggery. But the easterly breezes that bring with them a dreadful stench lead you to wonder about the meaning of 'minimal disease'. Recently you have heard that the piggery is to become free range. Pigs running everywhere! Maybe even on your property. How can this situation be resolved?

- As a timber worker, the activities of the 'greenies' have become a daily threat to your family's financial survival. Recently sugar was poured into your tractor's petrol pump, causing you considerable expense and loss of wages. Revenge is on your mind, but your conscience won't let you take action. What sort of action do you take?

★ A generalisation is a statement made about a whole group, based on knowledge of one member of that group.

★ Simple generalisations can be true and accurate, but often the evidence on which they are based is too limited for the statement to be convincing.

★ The more evidence you have to support your generalisation, the more believable it will be.

★ The language of a generalisation can be modified to make the statement more accurate.

★ Complex generalisations, which often contain value judgements, can be difficult to support. They require thought and careful consideration of supporting evidence.

4

Audience and purpose

Who are they? What is it?

All the world's a stage…

Shakespeare, *As You Like It*

Public speakers, teachers, advertisers, writers, students and politicians all need to be aware of the audience before them and their purpose in communicating with this group. The reason? So they know how best to convey their message.

Knowing your audience and purpose will help you to decide whether you should write a letter, a poem, a script, a formal essay, or in some other format. It will also enable you to choose the most appropriate language. For example, it would be inappropriate to deliver a complex political speech to a group of ten year olds. They simply wouldn't understand the language. The style of writing you choose — that is, the way you put your sentences together and the words and sounds that you use to create an impact — will vary according to the audience and purpose.

Audience and purpose

Your audience is the person or group of people to whom you are directing your message. In order to communicate effectively, it is essential to keep your audience in mind at all times. If you lose your sense of audience, the direction of your argument will be lost. Be clear about who you are writing for — children, adults, politicians, doctors, musicians, athletes — and develop your argument appropriately.

When writing on issues about which people hold many different views, your purpose is to persuade your audience to believe in *your* point of view. Every issue has two or more sides, and your purpose will vary according to the nature of the audience and the side that you support. For example, if the issue was capital punishment, your purpose in writing to a judge might be to convince him or her that the community wants to see that justice has been delivered following a murder or other serious crime. If you were against capital punishment, however, you might write a letter to the editor of a paper, with the purpose of persuading the public that life imprisonment is a more enduring, yet humane, form of punishment. Different audience, different purpose.

Writing to suit

When beginning to write on an issue, it might be useful to think in this way:
    Audience = WHO
    Purpose = WHY
    Writing = HOW

If you know you are writing for an audience of skateboarding teenagers, for example, you will write in a way that will interest, and therefore influence, that audience. If, on the other hand, you know you are writing for a group of Japanese businesspeople touring Australia you will use language convincing to them. Think about *who* makes up your audience and how you can best communicate with them. It is important to understand the needs and interests of your audience before you begin.

It is also important to know *why* you want to influence or persuade your audience. If you want to change the location of a skateboarding ramp, for instance, you must convince the teenagers who use it that they will not be disadvantaged by this. Similarly, if you want to encourage the Japanese businesspeople to invest in Australian property, you will need to persuade them of the benefits they would receive.

How you choose to write is up to you, and there are a number of ways open to you. You could write, for example, a humorous conversation between two people, a serious argumentative essay, a letter, a speech, a play, a television script or an advertising campaign.

Time to think

1 Can you add more to the list of writing styles above?
2 Which methods would you use for the skateboarding teenagers and for the Japanese businesspeople?

Recognising audience and purpose

The chart below lists a variety of audiences and purposes for three different topics.

Topic	Audience	Purpose
Conservation	Timber workers	To demonstrate the harm logging causes to the environment
	A kindergarten class	To show the children how they can care for the environment
	A gathering of elderly citizens	To convince them to help educate young people on caring for the environment
Television violence	The Censorship Board	To persuade its members to eliminate violence from children's shows
	Your parents	To convince them that Bugs Bunny cartoons contain no violence
	Film producers	To persuade them that screen violence encourages violence in the community
Sport	A group of parents	To convince them not to use negative language at their children's sporting competitions
	Your parents	To persuade them of the benefits to you of doing more sport
	A group of friends	To convince them to become involved in sport

Time to think

1 Using the above chart as a guide, think of three audiences and three purposes for three of the following topics.

- Graffiti
- Drugs
- The fashion industry
- Rollerblading
- Food

2 Choose one of the topics from the first list of topics, audiences and purposes above and write a response. You will need to decide on the writing style that best suits your audience and purpose — it could be a letter, a poem, an advertisement or a formal essay.

3 Write a response to one of the topics in the second list, for which you have decided on an audience and purpose.

Flashback

★ **Audience refers to the group of people to whom your message is directed.**

★ **Purpose refers to your reason for communicating your message to this group.**

★ **The success of any persuasive piece of writing depends on the writer's understanding of audience and purpose.**

★ **The style in which you choose to write will vary according to your audience and purpose.**

5

I contend that...

Establishing a viewpoint

I can never bring you to realize the importance of sleeves, the suggestiveness of thumbnails, or the great issues that may hang from a bootlace.

Sir Arthur Conan Doyle

28   Thinking critically

There is the possibility of an issue even in the most unlikely of places and human beings can create an issue out of almost anything. An issue is a subject on which there is a variety of views and on which disagreement may arise. As the world is made up of people of many different backgrounds and beliefs, it is not surprising that issues appear all around us. For example, when two or three people hold different views on the use of kangaroo meat as pet food an issue is created. A farmer whose crops are being destroyed by kangaroos might support the idea. A conservationist, who wants to protect native fauna, would probably argue against it.

Finding a viewpoint

Issues arise out of a variety of circumstances and can affect small or large numbers of people. The issue of teenage drinking and driving can have an effect on teenagers, their parents and innocent victims of accidents. The issue of nuclear energy can have an effect on whole populations or have global consequences.

The issues that surface daily in newspapers and on television can affect us directly or indirectly. It is human nature to express a viewpoint on the issues around us, regardless of whether or not we are affected by them.

Time to think

1 Here are some headlines that could appear in newspapers and magazines. Identify the issue contained within each headline and express your point of view on it.

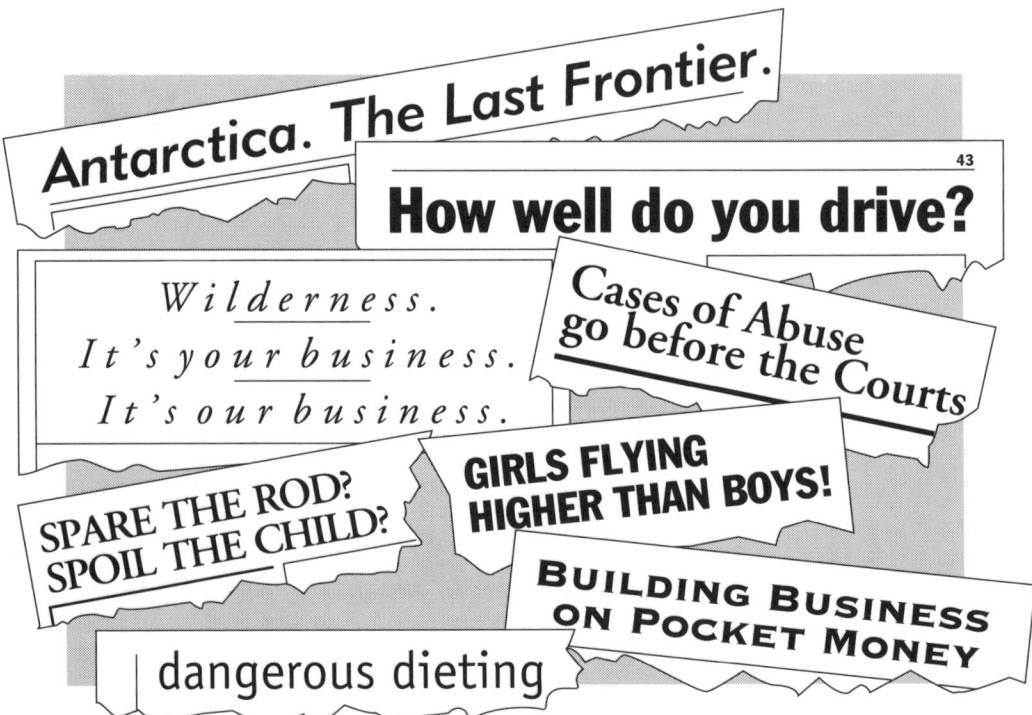

2 Think about some issues that might affect your life. Select five and write a newspaper headline for each. Make sure your headlines express a point of view.

Contentions

Within every issue is a contention. This is a statement expressing either support for, or opposition to, a particular aspect of an issue. The introductory paragraph of a persuasive or argumentative piece of writing expresses the writer's contention. In other words, it must be made very clear which side of the issue the writer supports. The contention expressed in the introductory paragraph must be developed and supported throughout a piece of writing, and each new paragraph must argue for that contention. (See also Chapters 6, 10 and 16.)

Consider the following example of an introductory paragraph on the topic, 'Our Kids Are Getting Fat'. The contention is underlined.

> **Just look around you! Look at what our kids are eating. How many chocolate ice creams, jam doughnuts and packets of chips has your child consumed this week? How much physical exercise has tested his or her miniscule muscles? <u>Poor diet and a lack of physical exercise are causing a generation of our children to expand unnecessarily and to experience the resulting ill-health.</u>**

Now consider this example, which examines the same issue from a different perspective. The writer is arguing for the opposing topic of 'Our Kids Are Becoming Too Thin'. The contention is underlined.

> **<u>Too many teenagers today are dieting to excess and are suffering extensive and damaging weight loss.</u> They are falling prey to the false images of advertising, and are trapped into believing that a slim body is the only beautiful body. Health, and a body which is breaking down, is disregarded in favour of the promises of success, in any area, that come from the tantalising images presented to the unsuspecting teenager.**

Time to think

1 Write introductory paragraphs for the topics 'Our Kids Are Getting Fat' and 'Our Kids Are Becoming Too Thin'. The idea expressed within each statement is the contention you must support. Use the paragraphs above as a guide.

Topic sentences

Each of the introductory paragraphs above contains a main sentence. That main sentence, which contains the contention, is also known as the topic sentence. When you are developing an argument, all subsequent paragraphs must also contain a topic sentence. It can appear anywhere within the paragraph, but it must be there.

Time to think

1 Find the topic sentences in the following two paragraphs.

> **If you don't have the time to care for a puppy, it's wise not to buy one. Too many puppies find their way to lost dogs' homes. Often they are in poor condition and staff find it necessary to put them down.**

> **Chocolate! White chocolate. Dark chocolate. Milk chocolate. The creaminess. The dreaminess. Originating from the humble cocoa bean, it has tempted taste buds for centuries. It has been pounded, powdered, melted, refined and consumed. The pleasure and the pain of it ensure human beings' enduring homage to chocolate, but it is bad for you.**

2 Select two of the following topics and write a paragraph on each. You can write on any aspect of the topic, but you must express an opinion. Another person might disagree with your view. Be careful to include a clear topic sentence (containing your contention), and remember that it can appear anywhere in the paragraph.
   - Capital punishment
   - Compulsory school sport
   - Compulsory school uniform
   - Using kangaroo meat as pet food

Compare your paragraphs with those of a friend. You will see that they are probably quite different.

Expressing your viewpoint

Here is a list of issues. Beside each are two statements of contention. The first expresses a point of view in support of an aspect of the issue; the second expresses a point of view against an aspect of the issue.

Issue	*Statements of contention*	
Smoking in public places	FOR	It is a person's right to smoke in public places.
	AGAINST	Smoking in all public places should be banned.
Violence on television	FOR	Violence on television has no harmful effects on children.
	AGAINST	Violence on television desensitises children and encourages aggression.
Fluoridation of water	FOR	Fluoridation of water is the answer to dental health.
	AGAINST	Fluoridation of water is bad for people's health.
Corporal punishment in schools	FOR	Corporal punishment is an effective form of discipline and should be re-introduced in all schools.
	AGAINST	Corporal punishment of children in schools is an archaic and ineffective form of discipline.

Time to think

1 Develop one statement of contention for and one against each of the following issues.
   - The legalisation of abortion
   - The individual's right to request euthanasia
   - The consequences of passive smoking
   - The use of performance-enhancing drugs by athletes
   - The design of the Australian flag

2 Newspapers and magazines keep you informed on what is happening in the world locally and overseas. Select two newspaper articles on local issues and two newspaper articles on overseas issues. Make sure you choose articles that express a point of view on an issue. Find and write down the contention of each article. Then write a paragraph expressing your own viewpoint on each issue. Remember that your paragraph should contain a clear statement of contention.

- ★ An issue is any subject on which there exists a variety of views and on which disagreement may arise.
- ★ It is natural to express a viewpoint on the issues that surround you.
- ★ A contention is a statement that expresses a viewpoint on a particular aspect of an issue.
- ★ A contention is the starting point for developing an argument.
- ★ In a persuasive piece of writing, each paragraph must contain a topic sentence that includes a contention.

6 Designing persuasive paragraphs

Essentials of a good paragraph

Just as the sentence contains one idea in all its fullness, so the paragraph should embrace a distinct episode; and as sentences should follow one another in harmonious sequence, so paragraphs must fit onto one another like the automatic couplings of railway carriages.

Winston Churchill

An essential ingredient of an effective piece of persuasive writing is the well-structured paragraph. No matter how creative or analytical the approach, the paragraph remains a vital building block in the construction of an argument.

Moving into, through and out of one paragraph and into, through and out of the next is a skill requiring much practice. If you are not sure why you are writing, or of how and when to start or finish a paragraph, your argument will become confused. Confusion can lead to paragraphs that lack direction and are disorganised. Before moving on to the elements that are common to all paragraphs, there are some concepts and key words that you need to understand.

What is persuasive writing?

The purpose of persuasive writing is to convince the reader to believe in a particular point of view, or to respond in a certain way. The world of advertising, for example, is well known for using language designed to persuade. (See Chapter 16.)

What is a paragraph?

Every paragraph in a piece of writing performs a particular function. The position of the paragraph within that piece of writing automatically gives it that function. These are the three different types of paragraphs with which you need to become familiar:

- the introduction
- the paragraph/s in the body of the piece of writing
- the conclusion

Each type follows a specific pattern. If all parts of the pattern are not included, the writing is incomplete and will read that way. The introduction establishes the contention and outlines the supporting arguments. The paragraphs in the body each contain one main point, a development of that point, and supporting evidence. The conclusion rounds off the point of view being expressed by summarising and restating the contention. It should be remembered that effective paragraphs usually contain three or more sentences to allow for a substantial discussion of the arguments. However, the length of introductions and conclusions can vary according to the way in which the writer wishes to convey the ideas.

The introduction

An introduction has a lot of work to do. It should

- clearly state the main contention;
- have a sense of belief in the point of view;
- use language that encourages the reader to continue reading;
- cause either agreement or disagreement in the reader;
- challenge the reader's established views and attitudes;
- use clear and accurate language; and
- outline the main arguments to be included in the body of the writing.

There are many ways to write an introduction. Each piece of writing will require a different approach, depending upon your audience, your purpose, and the structure of your argument. Here are some ideas on shaping an introduction that you might find useful.

- start or end with a question (see Chapter 16)
- start or end with a quotation
- use a question and a quotation
- use an anecdote (story)
- provide some interesting and relevant background
- include some emotional content
- include an interesting fact
- follow a number of short sentences with a longer sentence
- quote an expert

Time to think

1 Here are some sample introductions. Look at them carefully and see if you can locate the contention and identify any of the techniques suggested above.
- Take care on the roads! That is the message from the Victoria Police. Weekend and holiday road tolls need to come down. How do we do this? Drive safely. Don't drink and drive. Take regular breaks when making long trips.
- A young man lies motionless, his body twisted, blood flowing on to the road. Images such as this confront us on our television screens too often in the nightly news. How do we educate our young to wear seat belts? Seat belts are essential.
- The Commissioner for Traffic wants driver-training standards to be improved. Skilful driving eludes our young. Once they are away from the

instructor's watchful eye they are on their own and filled with false confidence. Rewarding the young for good driving would be an advantage.
- The national Easter road toll this year was 30. Sixteen of those killed were from New South Wales. What is happening in that State? Driver education, particularly for holiday periods, must be improved.
- 'Concentrate or kill.' These words, part of the Victorian road-safety advertising campaign, must not be taken lightly. Causing the death of someone on the road should be regarded as a crime. There must be some form of justice available for those innocent people killed, or maimed for life, on the State's roads.

2 Choose a topic from the list below. Write two introductions using some of the techniques suggested above. You will need to decide whether you are for or against the topic and express a clear point of view on it.
- The idea of recreating dinosaurs is ridiculous.
- Chewing gum in class alleviates boredom.
- Girls learn more easily in a single-sex classroom.
- Boys learn more easily in a single-sex classroom.

Body paragraphs

The paragraphs in the body of a persuasive piece of writing must seek to expand on the contention stated in the introduction. This requires careful paragraph structuring. A well-structured paragraph usually includes three or more sentences that express and develop one main idea. These sentences should include:

- a topic sentence expressing the main idea (usually the first sentence in a paragraph), but it can appear elsewhere;
- one or more sentences developing and discussing the idea;
- supporting evidence;
- convincing language;
- a commitment to the contention; and
- language that links one idea or sentence to the next.

With practice and confidence a writer will experiment with variations to this structure. For example, an experienced writer might start with the evidence and finish with the topic sentence. Paragraph structure can become more interesting and adventurous when extra thought is given to the presentation of ideas.

When you are first practising paragraph writing, however, it is best to follow a simple structure, as does the following example.

> **Chewing gum is not good for you. This is a scientifically established fact. When you chew gum your brain sends a message to the stomach that you are going to swallow something. The stomach prepares itself to receive food. When you don't swallow, the stomach compensates by eating a very tiny part of the wall of the stomach. Not a very pleasant idea!**

In this paragraph there is a logical sequence to the flow of ideas. Each sentence builds on or explains the previous sentence. The first sentence, which clearly states the contention, or main idea, is the topic sentence; the second, third and fourth sentences develop the main idea; the fifth sentence provides the evidence; and the final sentence provides a reaction to the subject. So, the writer has stated a clear view against chewing gum, has set about proving this viewpoint, and has included the supporting evidence.

Time to think

1 Select one of the four topics listed below and complete the tasks that follow.
   Republicanism would be good for Australia.
   Parents should be allowed to take their babies into restaurants.
   Video arcades! The adolescent's haven.
   Computer games will never replace a good old-fashioned tennis ball.
   - Write four different topic sentences for your selected topic. Before you write, decide whether you agree or disagree with the topic. In other words, know your contention before you begin.
   - Now select one of your four topic sentences and develop it into a paragraph that would fit into the body of a piece of writing. Use the above paragraph on chewing gum as a guide.

The conclusion

The final and most lasting impression you will have on your readers will come through your conclusion. So make it good. Remember that when you are writing persuasively your intention is to convince the reader that your views are strong, logical, thoughtful, easily understood, and worthy of consideration. The conclusion must be effective in drawing together your ideas and emphasising your contention.

There are many ways to write a conclusion. Here are some suggestions that might be helpful.

- Use language that has a 'finished' sound.
- Restate the viewpoint expressed in the contention.
- Use a concise concluding sentence.
- Use a question as the final sentence.
- Use a quotation as the final sentence.
- Draw together the arguments expressed.
- Include a final piece of startling information.
- Provoke thought in the reader.
- Choose either a short, sharp conclusion or a long, detailed one.

Time to think

1 Identify the different techniques used in these conclusions.
- Why is a dark tan no longer the fashion? Answer this yourself. What would you prefer? A healthy skin, or, perhaps, a shortened life?
- Our challenge in the issue of Australia's flag is to ensure that all people are represented by it. We are one nation. We are many different people.
- To repeat, equality of education must be available to all. Society cannot make distinctions based on gender, cultural background, skin colour, or disability. Education is for all.
- There is a spooky feeling about recreating the dinosaur. Scientists involved might become too advanced for technology and start to revive humans who had died. Imagine a recreated Adolf Hitler. While there is a humorous side to this issue, sanity must surface. In the hands of disturbed individuals, science could go sadly astray. The dinosaur must be left in the prehistoric period, not brought in to the world of today. Within hours of resurrection, destruction would be rampant.
- We must all be aware of the need to recycle. Recycling garbage is just one way in which we can help to ease the destruction of our natural resources. 'Electricity from rubbish?' Why not!

2 Choose another topic from the list of four provided on page 37 and write two conclusions using some of the techniques suggested above.

The language of links

Showing the connection between sentences and paragraphs can be difficult. The English language, however, provides many words that simplify this task. Familiarise yourself with the following transition or linking words and phrases and use them in your writing.

nevertheless	therefore
although	similarly
however	considering this
on the other hand	thus
despite this	according to
fortunately	unlike
in addition	eventually
generally	moreover
alternatively	importantly
while	significantly

Time to think

1 Copy the above list into your book and add your own words and phrases to it.
2 Consider the following two sentences.

> **Cows produce a considerable amount of manure.**
> **Cows can't fly.**

Although both sentences concern cows, there seems little else to link them. They are separate points. If a linking word is added, the two sentences start to establish a common theme.

> **Cows produce a considerable amount of manure.**
> **Fortunately, cows can't fly.**

Using this example as a guide, write ten pairs of seemingly unconnected sentences and then make connections using linking words from the above list.

- ★ **Persuasive writing is designed to persuade an audience to believe in a particular point of view.**
- ★ **Well-structured paragraphs are essential ingredients in effective persuasive writing.**
- ★ **Every paragraph within a persuasive piece of writing — introduction, body paragraphs, conclusion — has a specific role to perform.**
- ★ **Paragraphs should be connected to one another through the use of linking or transition words and phrases.**

7 Skilful summaries

Effective summary techniques

Let us try to reduce it to its bare essentials.

Common saying

A summary is a shortened version of any written or spoken material. It includes the main points or views expressed, necessary supporting evidence, and conclusions reached.

A summary can be a useful way to condense a long, detailed argument into a brief, easy-to-follow format. An effective summary allows you to

- distinguish essential from inessential information;
- understand a person's attitude to a subject;
- discover your own view on a subject; and
- speak and write more accurately.

Summarising techniques are used by many different people in many areas of life. These include:

- Students
- The third speaker in a debate
- Judges in court cases
- Writers of book or film reviews
- Editorial writers
- Journalists out on assignment
- Politicians at election time
- Television news reporters
- Writers of travel brochures

Writing a summary

A summary can be presented in point form, where only the main points are included in brief. It can also be presented as a paragraph containing fluent, structured sentences. If presented as a paragraph, the material should appear as a 'report' of what has been said or written. It should

- include the main points covered;
- link the main points to one another;
- exclude unnecessary facts and figures; and
- be written from the third-person point of view.

For example, a politician will deliver a speech using the first person, *I* and *we*. To summarise this speech, you, the reporter, would use the third person, *she*, *he*, *they*, or a person's name.

The following extract, written in the first person, is from Winston Churchill's wartime speech to the House of Commons in Britain:

> You ask what is our policy? I will say: It is to wage war, by sea, land and air, with all our might and with all the strength that God can give us: to wage war against a monstrous tyranny, never surpassed in the dark, lamentable catalogue of human crime. That is our policy. You ask, What is our aim? I can answer in one word: Victory — victory at all costs, victory in spite of all terror, victory, however long and hard the road may be . . .

Using the third person, the extract can be summarised as shown below. Notice that the speaker's name, Winston Churchill, has replaced the use of *I*.

> **Winston Churchill's wartime policy was to wage war in whatever way possible and to aim for victory no matter what.**

An article written in the third person should still be summarised in the third person. The following paragraphs on the issue of marijuana use are from an article, 'The Medical Outcome, Thirty Years of Cannabis Use', by Dr Giselle Cook (*Simply Living*, March 1994).

> One researcher reported twelve cases of advanced head and neck cancer in young marijuana users with an average age of 26. All had been daily marijuana and hashish smokers since high school, but did not smoke much tobacco or drink much alcohol.
>
> Another researcher found that seven out of the ten patients under the age of 40 with cancer of the respiratory tract he studied smoked marijuana daily.
>
> *Simply Living*, **March 1994**

These paragraphs can be summarised as follows:

> **Researchers have identified high incidences of certain types of cancer among young people who smoked marijuana on a daily basis.**

When summarising the opinions of other people it is useful to use the past tense rather than the present tense. For example, *is* becomes *was*, *are* becomes *were*, *has* becomes *had*, and so on.

Time to think

1 Test your own skills. Summarise the views expressed in the following letter written by 11-year-old Katrina Hansen. Find the contention first, then locate the supporting arguments.

> *Concerns for Wildlife*
> Why, oh why, must we kill the great masters of the ocean? Isn't steak good enough for the Japanese and Norwegians? If they sign a treaty, what will happen after the treaty is broken? Questions for the future.
>
> Will there be a future for these great beasts? I love these animals and I am sure many other people do. Fortunately there is a

sanctuary for them. But shouldn't all the seas of the world be one big sanctuary where they cannot be hunted for cosmetics and meat?

We must consider the people of younger generations who are hopefully smarter than the people who are causing deaths of all kinds of sea creatures. These creatures must be there for all generations to see.

If all whales are hunted out, other animals will die, for they rely on whales to bring up swirling food via their great power. We must be aware.

2 You have just read one person's view on whaling, but you might have a different one. In point form, summarise your view on whaling. Write down your contention and then give your reasons for holding that view.

3 The article below, 'Digital Photomontage' (*Scientific American*, February 1994), raises the question of how much we can trust photographic evidence. Read it and summarise in point form the ways in which you can tell that the accompanying photograph is a fake.

Digital Photomontage

Digital photomontage of seven astronauts on the surface of the moon was produced from an original photograph made in 1969 by NASA of a single astronaut, Edwin F. Aldrin, Jr. This montage is of high technical quality; it is carefully contrived to seem spatially consistent, and sophisticated digital technology has eliminated any obvious signs of cutting and pasting. So how can we tell it is a fake?

(*continued*)

There is an obvious internal inconsistency. Because the composition was produced from scaled-down replicas of the original figure, the reflections in the visors are incorrect. Each shows the image of just one other astronaut, not the several we would expect.

There is implausible repetition – good grounds for suspecting the image was produced by replication operations. Is it likely that all the astronauts except one would be holding their left arms in precisely the same position?

There are some questionable cast shadows. The artist had to insert these with a digital 'paintbrush' and faced the difficult task of making them consistent with the rough terrain. Do those at the back stand up to close, critical inspection?

Such flaws and inconsistencies are very obvious once they have been pointed out, but they often go unnoticed at first glance. A skilled forger attempts to anticipate the types of cross-checking that a suspicious viewer will perform, then adjusts the visual evidence accordingly.

4 Increasingly, the media is exposing us to constructed photographic images. In other words, editing techniques are used to create a photograph that might be the result of two or three separate photographs being cut and pasted together to create a new, but false, image. In one to three paragraphs, summarise your view on why the media manipulates the images it presents to us.

5 Read the article, 'Wake up to the New South Africa' (*Age*, 21 May 1994) on page 45, and using summary techniques, explain in fluent sentences what Satour believes it can help you to learn about the new South Africa.

6 Imagine you are a judge in a courtroom. You have just passed a judgement against a paper manufacturing company for polluting a nearby river. Summarise your attitude towards the company.

7 A friend has asked you for your opinion on a particular film that he or she wants to see. Select a film from those currently showing and write a letter to your friend about it. If you are making a positive recommendation, summarise the reasons why it is worthwhile seeing the film. If you did not enjoy the film, summarise the reasons why your friend should not see the film. You do not need to provide lengthy explanations in your summary.

8 Imagine that you are part of an editorial team for a daily newspaper. The subject for today's editorial is household rubbish and the issue of its disposal. Summarise your views on rubbish, then join with three or four other students in the class to write an editorial comment. You will need to combine each person's summarised views.

Wake up to the new South Africa

There's a new spirit in the land. A new nation has been born. It's a dynamic, historic time - with many people of goodwill working together towards the future. Experience this land where ecology is part of the culture. A land of huge vistas, exotic peoples, amazing fauna and flora. Now's the time to show your commitment - to see this magnificent country. And, in years to come, you'll be able to say, 'I was there'. Satour can help you. We're the authority on South Africa. It's our job to know the tours, business contacts, flora, fauna, topography, climate.

9 As a new writer for Getset, an expanding travel agency, your first assignment is to write a brochure on Alice Springs and Uluru. You have been instructed to write with American tourists in mind, and to ensure that your readers will gain an understanding of sacred Aboriginal sites. Summarise the key points to include.

- ★ **A summary is a shortened version of any written or spoken material and should include the main points and conclusions.**
- ★ **Summarising is a useful way to gain an overview of a writer's approach to an issue and is a skill that can be used in many different situations.**
- ★ **A summary can be written in point form or as a paragraph reported from the third-person point of view.**

8

Every effect has a cause

Understanding their relationship

To prove the effects of any particular kind of work is difficult . . .

Raymond Williams, *Communications*

Every effect has a cause

Every effect has a cause. An effect is a result or consequence produced by the action of someone or something. A cause is something that produces an effect on someone or something.

The words below are from the song 'MMM MMM MMM MMM' by Crash Test Dummies and they have been labelled as either cause or effect, where appropriate.

Once there was this kid
Who got into an accident **(Cause)**
and couldn't come to school. **(Effect)**

But when he finally came back
His hair had turned from black into bright white **(Effect)**
He said that it was from when
The cars had smashed so hard. **(Cause)**

Once there was this girl who
Wouldn't go and change with the girls in the change room **(Effect)**
But when they finally made her
They saw birthmarks all over her body **(Cause)**

Time to think

1 The next verse in the song describes another situation involving a child. With a partner see if you can work out the causes and the effects.

> *. . . then, there was this boy whose*
> *Parents made him come directly home right after school*
> *And when they went to their church*
> *They shook and lurched all over the church floor*
> *He couldn't quite explain it*
> *They'd always just gone there.*

2 Read all three verses of the song again. Label each of the causes as either *emotional* or *physical* causes. Emotional causes are those affecting the mind or relating to feelings in some way. Physical causes relate to objects having an impact on a body.

3 In the song the following lines come after the second verse:

> *But both girl and boy were glad*
> *'Cause one kid had it worse than that*

Why do you think the child in the last verse is described as having 'had it worse' than the other two?

4 Write down three situations that you think could be expressed as causes and effects.

Establishing the cause of the effect

Why worry about causes and effects? What purpose do they have in our lives? Where do we use them? The reasoning involved is used in a variety of real-life situations. For example, scientists use the logical process of looking at causes and effects in their experiments; doctors hold post mortems in order to determine the cause of death; police examine evidence such as fingerprints to make a charge against a person. So, thinking about causes and effects helps to solve many problems in everyday life.

In attempting to understand any situation or any argument, it is useful to ask yourself, 'What has happened that has caused this subject to be a point for discussion?' For example, the discovery of a dead dolphin on a beach leads a conservationist to wonder about the cause of death. This results in a post-mortem being conducted. The post-mortem finds a plastic bag caught in the dolphin's throat. This discovery is reported in the newspapers, which leads to conservation groups commencing a campaign against the use of plastic bags. Angry plastic-bag manufacturers claim that it is not the plastic bags that are the problem, but the people who use them. This causes two things. First, letters appear in the daily newspapers from people explaining how they dispose of or recycle their plastic bags and suggesting that others should follow their example. Second, local community groups organise a massive clean-up of drains, waterways and beaches. One incident has resulted in a sequence of causes and effects.

Time to think

1 Using the example above as a guide, design your own sequence of causes and effects based on the incidents listed below.
- Your friend has been accused of stealing a book from another student's locker.
- You have been suspended from school for three days for writing graffiti on the school walls.
- You are in need of some extra money. You manage to find a part-time job at a local restaurant. After working there for a number of days you realise that this is the job that your friend just lost.
- Your sister has won a scholarship to study overseas.

In the news

Newspaper and television journalists report the causes and effects occurring around us each day.

Time to think

1 Read 'Earthweek: Diary of a Planet' (*Age*, 7 June 1994) by Steve Newman. Write down the cause and effect identified under each heading.

Earthweek: Diary of a Planet

Killing heat

The most searing heatwave to strike India and Pakistan in 50 years has killed hundreds of people and worsened the water shortage in several metropolitan areas. The mercury soared to 49 degrees Celsius across India's western state of Rajasthan and parts of neighboring Pakistan.

Dust storm

A huge dust storm raging across southeastern Australia blew an estimated 30 million tonnes of soil out to sea and blanketed Sydney and other cities in a thick brown haze. The storm, described as a disaster by environmentalists and farmers, was about 700 kilometres wide and 200 kilometres long at its height.

Earthquakes

A moderate quake registering a magnitude of 4.5 wrecked homes in the Andean regions of Venezuela and Colombia, but there were no reports of serious injuries. A swarm of tremors rumbled beneath the Strait of Gibraltar, with the strongest damaging several homes and killing one child at Al Hoceima, Morocco. Earth movements also were felt in Burma, central Japan and Southern California.

Senegal storms

Violent tropical thunder-storms across eastern Senegal inflicted extensive damage and killed two people with lightning bolts.

Whale slaughter

During a week when a massive whale sanctuary was established in the southern oceans and the worldwide moratorium on whaling was renewed, police in the Philippines were reported to have slaughtered a beached whale and allowed villagers to feast on its carcase. The officers sprayed automatic rifle fire into the stranded mammal, then the villagers hacked it into pieces, which they ate in a giant festival.

Drought

A prolonged drought in Puerto Rico has depleted lakes and forced water rationing on nearly half the residents of the island. Lakes serving as sources of fresh water have shrunk, with one reservoir hitting its lowest recorded level. Cardinal Aponte Martinez urged all Christians to pray for rain.

Monkey menace

Vigilante groups armed with bows and arrows hunted a marauding monkey that has slapped, bitten and scratched scores of people in Bangladesh, putting 13 of them in hospital.

(*Additional Sources:* Indian Weather Bureau, US Climate Analysis Centre, Us Earthquake Information Centre and the World Meteorological Organisation.)

2 Read 'The Greenhouse Effect on Life on Earth' (*Age*, 7 June 1994) by Steve Malcolm and answer the questions below and on page 51.
- Refer to the diagram and the written material and list those activities that cause the release of gases and contribute to the greenhouse effect.
- Why should we understand the greenhouse effect on life on earth?
- Why has the writer included so many facts in his article? (You will need to recall why facts are important in developing persuasive arguments. See Chapter 2.)

The Greenhouse Effect on Life on Earth

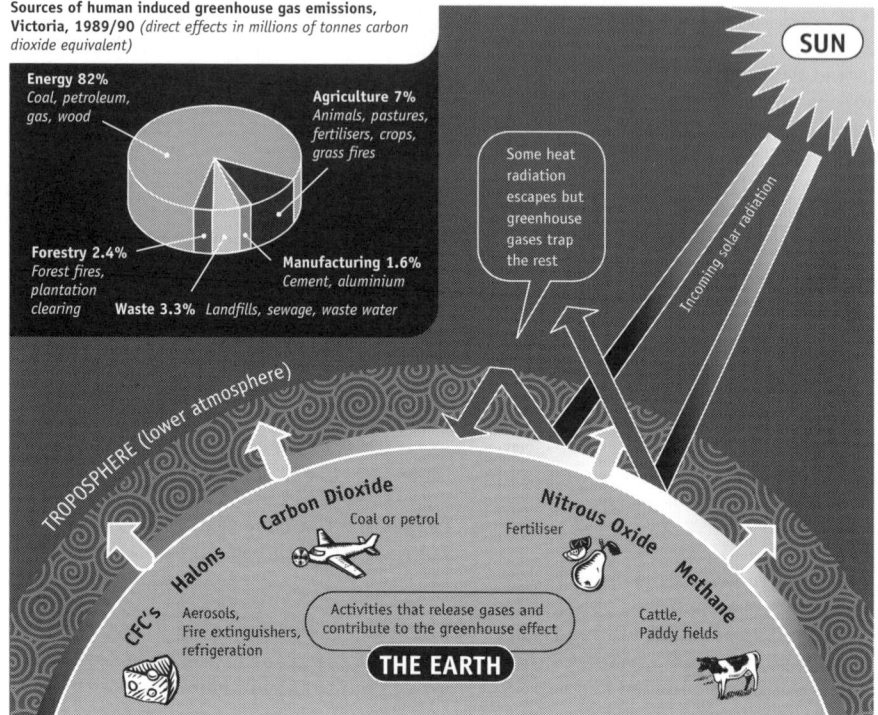

The earth's atmosphere acts like a greenhouse by trapping the warming energy from the sun. This helps maintain the earth's surface at temperatures that are necessary for the survival of present forms of life.

Human-caused changes to the composition of the atmosphere since the Industrial Revolution have raised serious concerns that the greenhouse effect is being artificially enhanced, raising the earth's temperature.

An increase in average temperatures of even a few degrees can have extremely serious environmental, social and economic impacts through the effects of raised sea levels and changed weather patterns.

In addition to naturally occurring gases like carbon dioxide, methane and nitrous oxide which have been increased by human activities, some artificial substances, notably chlorofluorocarbons (CFCs) and halons, also contribute to global warming.

Burning fossil fuels for energy is an important source of greenhouse gases. For example, the use of petrol in cars and coal-sourced electricity in homes and businesses releases vast amounts of carbon dioxide and other greenhouse gases into the atmosphere.

With a little thought, each person can find ways to reduce use of energy from fossil fuels. It is important to remember that the effectiveness of recently agreed national and international greenhouse response strategies depends heavily upon individual action and community encouragement for strong, continuing efforts by government and industry.

- The article says that, 'With a little thought, each person can find ways to reduce use of energy from fossil fuels.' Find out the meaning of fossil fuels and the greenhouse effect, then list things that individuals can do to help reduce the greenhouse effect.
- Discuss with a partner how you might currently be affected by the greenhouse effect? Write your answer as a cause, then as an effect.

3 Read 'Never Give Up, Says An Angel Named Henry' (*Age*, 7 June 1994) by Martin Flanagan and answer the questions that follow.

Never Give Up, Says An Angel Named Henry

The woman is drunk. 'I wouldn't be like this if it wasn't for him, Henry,' she says, referring to her uncontrollable 15-year-old son.

Henry Nissen takes her arm. He is delivering fruit and vegetables he has scrounged from South Melbourne Market. 'But two wrongs don't make a right, Mary,' he says in his soft, slightly muffled voice.

A girl, perhaps five, stands beside her mother in the bare, unlit flat, playing with her bangles.

Henry Nissen is a small man with bright eyes and a bent nose. He smiles a lot. People hail him as he passes – a Greek boy whose brother died last year of an overdose, three street kids from Western Australia.

He gives the street kids an accommodation voucher for a night in a St Kilda boarding house. 'Most kids aren't on drugs when they start on the streets,' he says. 'But they are by the end.' He urges the Greek boy to stick with football.

He holds people when he speaks to them. The guilty whisper in his ear and look furtively over his shoulder. His parting words to them all are the same. 'Love and best wishes,' he says.

Finally, back in his vehicle, he answers his beeper – not one message awaits him, but 13. 'There's never enough time,' says Henry Nissen. Sweat drips from his nose.

His body, as befits a former flyweight boxer, is light and strong. Henry Nissen won the Australian professional flyweight title in his third fight, the Commonwealth crown in his ninth. He was offered a shot at the world title before he felt he was ready. When he was ready, the offer didn't come. He was heart-broken. He even went to Italy seeking the fight, but to no avail.

He still thinks about what might have been and, with a little prompting, can be cajoled into reliving old fights. Twice he was put down in the fourth round by world-rated opponents. On both occasions, he got up and won. 'You never give up,' he says. 'That's the end.'

Henry Nissen says boxing is a brutal sport, but it has a place. One of the people he has co-opted into helping Open Family, the foundation for which he works, is Jeff Fenech. He describes Fenech as a street kid who has come a long way.

Another person who helped was John Bell. 'He never let me down,' he says.

Henry Nissen spent parts of his childhood in institutions, because of a recurring illness suffered by his mother. He was exposed to street violence at an early age. His first response was to join a gang, but when he saw what the gang did he tried to change them.

'Why attack someone who's on their own,' he said. 'That's a mongrel act. If you want to test your courage, fight one-out.' Once he even offered to fight on a

(*continued*)

victim's behalf. Along with his twin brother, Leon, he also took up boxing.

It was after he had returned from Italy, having failed to arrange a world title fight, that he chanced upon a copy of Erich von Daniken's 'Charlots of the Gods'. The book intrigued him. In 1980, he travelled to India and, in the Madras compound of the sage Krishnamurti, attended a conference of the World Theosophist Society and was persuaded that all religions are ultimately one.

When he returned from India, he used the money he had made from boxing, bought a house and converted it into a halfway home. 'Henry,' he was told, 'you should look after your own family first.'

'All people are my family,' he replied.

Henry Nissen believes that life is ultimately a journey of the spirit. He believes in astral travelling and out-of-body experiences. 'The more conscious you become,' he says, 'the less selfish you are.'

He recently explained the principle of reincarnation, of a justice beyond this life, to a 15-year-old charged with murder. The youth listened.

Some people say Henry Nissen is mad. Others say that he's a saint. He laughs, as if to say anything's possible. 'It may be that all the books I've read are wrong, that all the learning I have acquired is false. But I still get strength from the giving.'

Last year, he helped a group of young skinheads find shelter. They thanked him for his help, and took him into their confidence. Have nothing to do with Asians, black and Jews, they told him. 'But I am Jewish,' he said.

He hasn't given up on them. Henry Nissen doesn't give up on anyone. Giving up, he says, is the end.

- What has caused Henry Nissen to help street kids?
- What effect has helping street kids had on Henry Nissen?
- Can you see any effect on those he has helped?
- Describe the effect of 'giving up'?
- The writer has chosen this subject as the first in an 'occasional series' of articles. What do you think may have caused him to do so?

4 Read the television news report below and answer the questions that follow.

SCENE 1: INT. NEWS DESK.   NIGHT.

NEWS READER: Homicide-squad detectives are seeking two youths over the death of a motorist on the eastern freeway yesterday. A middle-aged man died after a rock smashed through his windscreen and hit him in the chest. Police believe it was thrown from an overpass and say several other cars were also hit.

CUT TO:

SCENE 2. EXT. CLIFTON HILL.   FREEWAY SITE OF ACCIDENT. PREVIOUS NIGHT.

POLICE REPORTER: At first police thought it was another tragic freeway crash. But they quickly discovered this was no accident. A man had been driving west along the Eastern Freeway yesterday afternoon when a rock was thrown at his car from the Yarra Bend overpass. It smashed through the windscreen striking him on the chest. His car careered across the road for a kilometre, eventually ramming another vehicle further down the freeway. The man died at the scene. It's believed he was killed by the rock, not the subsequent accident.

CUT TO:

SCENE 3. INT.

HOMICIDE SQUAD REPRESENTATIVE: It's quite a callous act and . . . total disregard for the safety and the welfare of the persons using the roadway . . .

CUT TO:

SCENE 4. EXT. FREEWAY. DAY.

POLICE REPORTER: Police say at least three or four other vehicles were struck by rocks around the same time. In one incident a thirteen-year-old boy travelling with his mother was struck on the head when a rock smashed through the car windscreen.

CUT TO:

SCENE 5. INT.

HOMICIDE SQUAD REPRESENTATIVE: Yes . . . extremely lucky he wasn't killed as well.

CUT TO:

SCENE 6. EXT. FREEWAY. DAY.

POLICE REPORTER: Two teenagers were seen throwing rocks from the overpass yesterday afternoon. Today police investigations focused on the bridge and surrounding bush- land. Because it's a homicide, the death isn't counted as part of a long-weekend road toll.

INT. = Interior
EXT. = Exterior
CUT TO = A quick change from one scene to another

- A number of causes and effects occur in this report. Working with a partner, read through each section of dialogue, and in two columns — one headed *causes*, the other *effects* — list as many causes and effects as you can find.
- Every incident (cause) has a consequence (effect). What possible consequences do you think might result from the incident discussed in this report?
- Write your own television news report based on one of the two incidents described below. You will need to use your imagination. Develop a number of imaginary facts then put them together using a cause and effect structure. Use the report above, which is written as a script and set out in scenes, as a guide.

  The body of a twelve-year-old boy is found outside an inner-suburban factory.

  Two sheep are found wandering around in the city centre.

- ★ An effect is an outcome produced by the action of someone or something.
- ★ A cause is something that produces an effect on someone or something.
- ★ Every effect has a cause.
- ★ Thinking in terms of causes and effects helps to address many of the problems you encounter in everyday life.

9

Just letting you know

Writing informatively

Still he hungered for more information

Frank Jacobs

Informative writing should communicate ideas, facts and details about an issue to an audience. When you write you collect all relevant information on the subject, then put it together so that the result serves a useful purpose for the reader. The most important feature of this style of writing is that it provides the reader with a body of knowledge that can become a springboard for discussion on an issue.

Writing to inform

When writing informatively on an issue you are writing about a subject on which there are two or more points of view. As you are writing informatively, your task is simply to tell your reader about one, two, or more of the points of view on the issue. There is no need to try to persuade. Your task is to provide the reader with *information*. Therefore, the writing needs to be unbiased. This means it should not favour one side of the issue over others.

Gathering the information

There are usually many sources of information on any issue you can think of. Your own memories and experiences are wonderful places to start, as are the resources listed below.

- Films, documentaries, television news, videotapes, audiotapes, computer networks
- People you know — friends, family, teachers
- People you don't know — experts on the subject
- Organisations associated with the issue
- Conversations you've had
- Reference books, newspapers, magazines
- Libraries and librarians

No matter how insignificant the information may seem, record it. Keep it for later. It might provide you with a perfect starting point or a perfect conclusion.

Presenting the information

Once you have gathered all of the relevant information, you need to communicate this information to your audience. Using more than one source of information serves two purposes. First, it enlarges the range of material, views and data you can present. Second, it identifies and counter-balances any biases that may be present in one specific source. It is important to remember that your audience has not had the opportunity to examine or consider these sources of information in the way that you have.

When your research is complete, the first step is to select the details from the source material that you wish to convey to your audience. There is a variety of ways to do this. These include providing

- a summary of the information in your own words;
- direct quotations, using the exact words of the original material;
- statistical details;
- results of surveys;
- descriptive details of people and places;

- anecdotes or stories of incidents or events;
- reports of experiences;
- extracts of interviews.

Whichever methods you use to inform your audience, the range of facts at your disposal should be communicated in a way that leads your reader to experience the same increase in knowledge that you have experienced in the collection of the information.

From the beginning, the purpose of your writing should be clear, as should the nature of the topic (see Chapter 4). The presentation of information must succeed with the audience, so the writing must be logical, structured and clear. Each paragraph should add to the body of information available to the reader. This is where your planning becomes important. Select the main points to be included, then work out the best order for the ideas. Each idea must build on the previous one. Each paragraph must contain a topic sentence, development of the point, and supporting examples (see Chapter 6).

Within this style of writing it is possible to adopt an approach other than the straightforward essay. Information can be presented in point form, or by using graphs and charts. Your language should be accurate and clear, and your sentences carefully structured.

The final paragraph in an informative piece of writing needs to include an evaluation of the subject on which you are writing. This is a comment that rounds off the material presented and provides a sense of completion. It is the place where you are able to make an observation on the subject.

This plan on the topic 'Homelessness in Australia' can be used as a guide for your own planning.

INTRODUCTION	Introduce the subject of homelessness and make a statement showing that homelessness is not confined to one group in society. Explain the meaning of 'homelessness'.
PARA 1	Topic sentence: The causes of homelessness are varied (e.g. loss of employment, lack of family support, psychological illness, etc.). This supports and develops the topic sentence.
PARA 2	Topic sentence: Homelessness is increasing. Use of census/survey data, newspaper reports, comments from welfare workers. This supports and develops the topic sentence.
PARA 3	Topic sentence: The nature of homelessness is changing. No longer old men on park benches. Now it can be young people, single-parent families, psychologically disturbed people previously in institutions. This supports and develops the topic sentence.
PARA 4	Topic sentence: Traditional responses cannot cope with the numbers. Salvation Army, overnight shelters, rooming houses, police cells are no longer appropriate. This supports and develops the topic sentence.
CONCLUSION	Evaluative comment: We need to find new ways of coping with homelessness.

Time to think

1 Write your own plan on one of the following topics.
   Taking Risks — To Do and Not To Do
   The Strain of Starting School

2 Read 'Nintendo and Epilepsy — The Links Explored' (*Nintendo Magazine System*, May 1993) and answer the questions that follow.

Nintendo and Epilepsy – The Links Explored

If you have been watching the news and reading the newspapers lately, the numerous stories linking Nintendo and Sega games and epileptics suffering seizures cannot have failed to catch your eye.

According to various reports, players already diagnosed as epileptics have been subject to fits after playing with their consoles. As people attempt to link the attacks to flashing sprites and on-screen effects, both Nintendo and Sega are being asked to print warnings regarding the alleged dangers.

Despite the current press hysteria regarding the links between video games and such seizures, the percentage of epilepsy sufferers prone to such attacks is very small.

> **Remember, if you are a worried epilepsy sufferer, try these tips:**
> • Stop playing immediately if you feel any discomfort at all.
> • Take a break from playing every now and again.
> • Don't sit too close to the screen.
> • It sounds silly, but wearing sunglasses while playing can also help if the screen is causing you some discomfort. Remember, if you still have any worries, consult with your doctor or call the Epilepsy Association in your State.

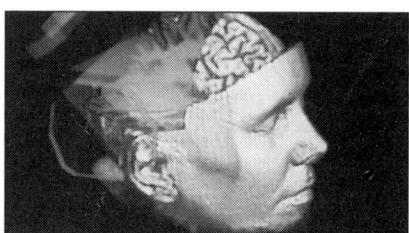

According to figures released by the British National Society For Epilepsy, one person in every 200 suffers from epilepsy, whilst the number of people susceptible to attacks brought on by photo-sensitivity – images from a television or indeed a flashing video game – make up three per cent of these sufferers. In other words, 0.015% of the population.

Meanwhile in Australia, the press seemed to have a lot to say on the matter though the idea of actually consulting any experts seemed to be well beyond them (otherwise known as The Royal Family Syndrome). So we thought we'd do it instead.

Having had a chat to epilepsy experts both in Australia and the UK, NMS advises that if you are a sufferer of epilepsy and are worried about any possible dangers of using your console, follow these guidelines:

(continued)

> While flashing lights or certain geometric patterns are among the environment that may very occasionally lead to a seizure, this is very rare, even in patients with known epilepsy. Now, there are many forms of such stimulation – the regular TV set being the most obvious – but it can also take the form of striped objects like zebra crossings and lines of trees, and not to forget computer material. While it is always sensible for the console user to take reasonable precautions – don't sit too close to the screen and use good background illumination – the risk should not be overplayed.
>
> The vast majority of epilepsy sufferers are not sensitive to these stimuli and should not be prevented from using consoles.
>
> There is no doubt that these attacks, when they occur, are very serious.
>
> However reason should prevail.

- What is the issue in this article?
- Look carefully at the language used in the article. It contains some key words and phrases that tell the reader what type of research has been conducted on this issue. For example, 'Having had a chat to epilepsy experts . . .' tells you that the writer has interviewed experts on epilepsy. List all the words and phrases that indicate the sources of information.
- What are the possible reasons that inspired this writer to prepare this article?
- The article appears in *Nintendo Magazine System — Australia's Only Guide to Game Boy, Nes, & Super Nes*. Who do you think is the audience for this article?
- What effect do you believe the article will have on that audience?
- The two features of this article that create extra interest and impact are the photograph and the box of 'tips'. What visual purpose do they serve?
- Why might the writer have chosen to present the information in the box in this way? Think about the impact on you as a reader.
- The final sentence in the article is an evaluative comment (see above). What information about the writer does the final sentence provide for the reader? Keep in mind your knowledge about bias.

Ways to inform

Informative writing can take various forms, as shown in the list below.

- A newspaper report
- Cartoons, photographs or charts supporting written material
- An interview
- A news report
- A comedy sketch
- A play
- A dialogue between two people who agree with one another
- A letter
- An essay
- A speech
- A poem or short story

Time to think

1 Collect two or three newspaper or magazine articles on the same issue that provide information on that issue. Look for articles that present the information in different ways, for example, using a cartoon, a photograph, a letter or a chart.
   - Which approach to the subject do you prefer?
   - Considering the different newspaper or magazine, who is the likely audience for each article?
   - Have the writers' approaches to their subjects been guided by their audience?
   - Is the material presented in a light-hearted, serious or humorous way?
   - Are the words and phrases used appropriate to the audience? That is, if the article is written for children, will they be able to understand it?
   - What do you think each writer's purpose is in writing the article?

Journalists as informers

Journalists write to provide information on a particular subject. Current affairs programmes and many newspaper articles result from the work of 'investigative' journalists. They usually have a particular purpose in mind, and select, from a wealth of available information, those details that they wish to convey to their audience.

Time to think

1 Take on the role of an investigative journalist. You will need to explore all aspects of an issue, using the research techniques outlined above, before writing your piece.
   - From the many newspapers and magazines available in your local newsagent, select one for which you are a writer. (Knowing the newspaper or magazine you are writing for will help you to know your audience.)
   - You have been asked to investigate an issue that is gaining a lot of media attention. You need to work out the issue and why it is attracting attention. This will help you understand your purpose.
   - Establish whether you are informing on one side of the issue, on both, or on a range of viewpoints on the issue. This will help you to know how much and what sort of information to collect.
   - What will be your approach to the issue? Use the list of 'Ways to inform' above as a guide. The decision on this might be best left till the research is completed.

Here is a list of topics from which to choose. If none of these suits you, make your own selection.
   - Man's threat to the survival of the panda.
   - Garbage as a source of fuel.
   - The arguments for and against euthanasia.
   - Robotics in the future.
   - The search to prove the existence of the Tasmanian Tiger.
   - The case for and against mandatory reporting of child abuse.
   - Homeless youth.
   - Provision of facilities for Australia's ageing population.
   - Males and females and how they use computers.
   - The impact of soap operas on the 'television generation'.

Once you have selected your topic you will need to work out how to start this project. These steps might be helpful:
   - Collect the information carefully and record it in an orderly way.
   - Think about the information. You might find that your original focus changes as you gather more information. Be prepared to alter your approach.
   - Find a logical and organised way of keeping all the snippets of information together.
   - Think about the evaluation. How will you construct this? Can you present a theory on the issue?
   - Remember that you are writing as a journalist and should report on the issue without showing any bias.
   - Think about your readers. The information you present must be useful for them.

When you have collected all available information, you are ready to write up your response. Decide on the best method of presentation. This is probably one of the most difficult decisions because it is where your individuality and creativity surfaces. Be sure to consider your audience and your purpose in writing. Allow yourself a limit of 500 to 600 words.

- ★ **Informative writing should communicate ideas, facts and details about an issue.**
- ★ **When writing informatively you should not be presenting your own view, but a range of different views on an issue.**
- ★ **Effective informative writing is based on thorough research, consideration of your audience and purpose, and clear presentation of material.**
- ★ **Your audience should experience the same increase in knowledge that you have in collecting all available information for your piece.**

10

Thoughts on paper

Argumentative writing

> There's nothing either good or
> bad but thinking makes it so.
>
> **Shakespeare,** *Hamlet*

In a formal argumentative essay the writer is expected to develop a viewpoint and to state clearly the evidence that supports that viewpoint. In doing so the writer is arguing a case. The presentation of that case should be as objective and free of bias as possible. This means that the viewpoint should be argued for, without allowing feelings to be introduced to weaken the argument.

It is appropriate in the formal essay to avoid writing from the first-person point of view. This means you should not use the personal pronoun *I*. In its place, you should write from the third-person point of view, using the personal pronouns *he*, *she* and *it*. This creates the distance and formality required of the argumentative essay.

In developing an argument, part of the task is to produce a set of reasons for the contention that can withstand the opposition. When you acknowledge an aspect of the opposing view, the purpose should be to strengthen your own view by underlining the weaknesses of your opponent's.

Argumentative essays

The terms used to describe the features of argumentative writing are outlined below.
- *Argument*   reasons for a point of view or an informed opinion
- *Counter argument*   the opposing argument
- *Contention*   the stance or position taken
- *Opinion*   a personal view held or a belief on a subject of dispute
- *Point of view*   a particular position on an issue
- *Issue*   a subject on which there are various points of view
- *Idea*   way of thinking or a thought
- *Development of an idea*   adding more information to a way of thinking or building up a stronger understanding of the thought
- *Topic sentence*   sentence in a paragraph that contains the main point for that paragraph
- *Supporting evidence*   factual details, examples, quoting of authorities, statistics, and other evidence
- *Rebuttal*   negation of counter argument to enhance own position
- *Objective language*   rational, clear, logical, impersonal words, phrases and sentences that are free of emotion
- *Subjective language*   words, phrases and sentences that express ideas based on personal experiences, feelings and emotions

Building argumentative essays

A formal argumentative essay should follow this pattern:
1. An *introduction* that clearly expresses the contention and outlines the main arguments to be included in the essay.
2. The *body* of the essay — usually four to five paragraphs, each containing an argument in support of the contention. Each paragraph must include a topic sentence containing the main idea. The idea must be developed and supported with evidence.

3 A *rebuttal*. While it is acceptable to include the rebuttal in one separate paragraph, placed immediately before the conclusion, it is preferable to include a rebuttal in each paragraph. This, however, involves more complex writing, and requires skill and practice.
4 The *conclusion*. This should be convincing and should emphasise the contention for which the writer has been arguing.

Time to think

1 With a partner establish contentions for and against the issues listed below. It is more usual to express an issue in the form of a statement, but for the purpose of this exercise they have been expressed as questions.
   - Should baby beauty contests be banned?
   - Can we trust the media to report news accurately?
   - Are we bringing up our children to be too materialistic?
   - Should we encourage more tourism to Australia?
   - Should driver education for students be a compulsory part of secondary education?
2 Discuss with a partner issues that might affect you, or that you are aware of around you. Write a list of five issues. Join with another two students to discuss both lists. Note how many issues you have in common. Discuss whether or not the things on your list are in fact issues (see Chapter 5). Establish within your group how many of you are *for* the issue and how many are *against*.
3 Read 'Parents Not Buying Ads for Children' (*Age*, 6 April 1994) and answer the questions that follow.

Parents not buying ads for children

Australian parents are becoming concerned about the amount of television advertising aimed at children.

More than two-thirds of parents surveyed in a new study by the Federal Bureau of Consumer Affairs said advertising led to materialistic values in children.

Parents with four or more children were extremely concerned about the pressure exerted on their families to buy and consume products.

Eighty per cent of parents interviewed in the survey said advertising directed at

(*continued*)

children put pressure on them to buy.

Yet the regulations for television advertising aimed at children, the Children's Television Standards, prohibit advertisements which lead to undue pressure being placed on parents.

A researcher for the Federal Bureau of Consumer Affairs, Ms Gayle Ovington, said it appeared that the Children's Television Standards were being breached.

Seventy-nine per cent of parents surveyed said there should be stricter controls on such advertising.

A total of 1301 parents were surveyed in the study.

Ms Ovington said the standards did not regulate the morning timeslot, from 7.30 am to 9 am, when children watched television. Another bureau survey showed that toys and junk food were advertised at this time and that as much as 27 per cent of the on-air time was advertising.

During this time programs such as 'Agro's Cartoon Connection' promoted products through the hosts, she said.

'The research shows that children under five cannot distinguish between advertisements and programs, so it is even more difficult to make a distinction if a presenter is involved in what is an advertisement,' Ms Ovington said.

If the morning programs were covered by the children's standards, it would be unlikely that the promotions and prizes would be allowed, she said.

- What is the contention in the article?
- What supporting arguments does the writer present?
- What are three different types of evidence used by the writer?
- Is the concluding paragraph effective? Does it make a strong point?
- What is your point of view on the issue presented in this article?

Writing effective arguments

For a piece of argumentative writing to be effective, some important points need to be observed (see also Chapters 3 and 6). These are:

- All opinions must be clearly supported with evidence (facts, statistics, examples).
- Avoid being emotional — this can destroy a strong argument.
- Organise your ideas — one idea should lead logically on to the next.
- Ensure that the introduction and the conclusion fulfil their roles.

Creating style

After observing the points listed above, turn your attention to your 'style'. Style refers to the way in which you put your ideas together and the language and sentence structure that you use. A strong, appealing style helps keep your audience interested. The points listed below will help you to develop an appropriate style.

- Have a belief in your argument and a commitment to your contention.
- Have confidence in your ideas throughout the piece by ensuring that they are well supported by evidence.
- Use clear and strong expression — look up key words in a thesaurus and produce a relevant vocabulary list before you start writing.

- Select your vocabulary carefully — avoid using lots of little words simply to pad out the word length of your piece.
- Consider using rhetorical questions to emphasise important points.
- Use a combination of long and short sentences.
- Avoid making personal attacks on people referred to in your argument.
- Avoid resorting to sarcasm to make your point.
- Keep a list of useful linking words handy (see Chapter 6).

Planning

When planning a piece of argumentative writing, you might choose the 'brainstorm' approach (see Chapter 12), or you might choose the 'straight up and down' ordering of ideas approach, as is shown in the example below. Whichever method you choose, a structure must be present in each paragraph and in the essay overall.

| TOPIC | 'Girls and playing cricket go well together' |

Introduction	State contention in support of proposal expressed in topic. Perhaps define proposal as applied to girls playing in mixed teams.
Next paragraph	First argument: Previously regarded as a male sport, to participate in it develops self-esteem for girls. Evidence: Girls feel positive about competing with boys. They are on the same level.
Next paragraph	Second argument: It helps girls to develop a team spirit. Evidence: Working in co-operation on strategies.
Next paragraph	Third argument: Girls have a chance to develop skills. Evidence: Hand/eye co-ordination, timing and strength.
Next paragraph	Rebuttal: While regarded as inhibiting males in their development, some development needs inhibiting. Evidence: Boys' behaviour and language is moderated.
Conclusion	Refer back to the original contention. Perhaps finish with a quotation.

Drafting

Part of the process of writing an essay includes going through the various stages of drafting. All writers' first drafts will need some changes. Two drafts are usually sufficient (a first and a final), but sometimes three are written.

Time to think

1 The following piece of writing by student Andrew Cameron includes a 'brainstorm' plan, one draft with handwritten corrections (done by the student), and a final draft. The title of the essay is 'Republicanism would be good for Australia' and the student has chosen to argue against the proposal. Read the drafts carefully and discuss the writing in small groups, using the following points as a guide.
   - Examine the clarity of the contention.
   - Consider the effectiveness of the introduction and the conclusion.
   - Look at the structure of the paragraphs.
   - Notice the use of any supporting evidence.
   - Analyse the persuasive techniques used (see Chapter 16).
   - Comment on the drafting process and the changes made to the first draft.

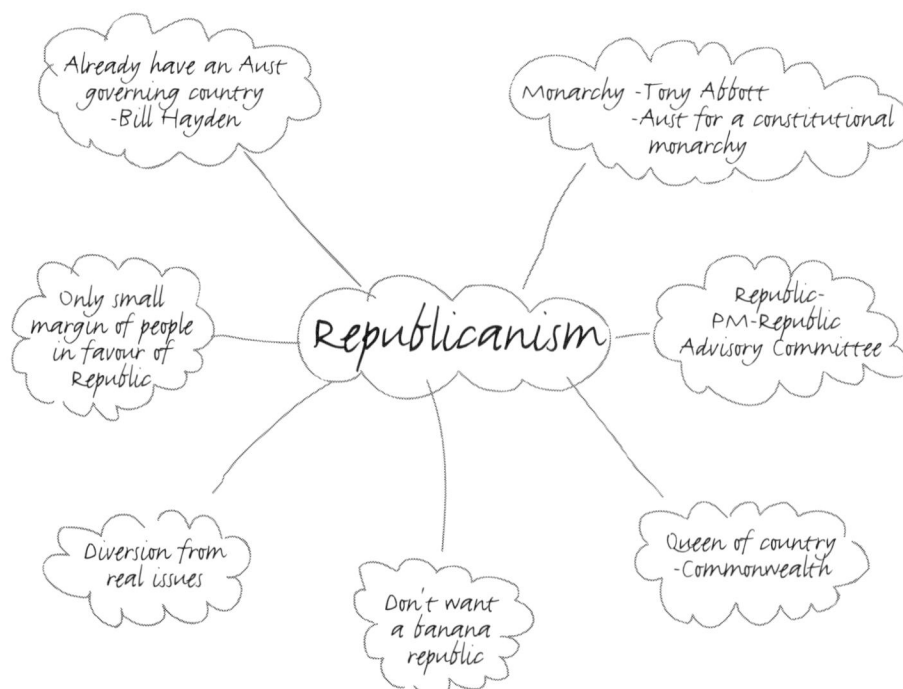

First draft

[margin: examples needed]
[margin top: not be - other motion]

REPUBLICANISM WOULD BE GOOD FOR AUSTRALIA

A republic would certainly not be good for Australia! ~~whatsoever!~~ Australia is a proud country; a country with a proud past as a constitutional monarchy and a proud future ahead of itself as part of the British monarchy and Commonwealth.

The strongest reason for Australia staying as a monarchy is that the monarchy creates stability between the government and its people. It also serves as a figurehead role.

Unfortunately, today the republic issue is being turned into a political diversion by the present Prime Minister. This diversion is a complete distraction from the main issues which we as Australians are facing. Environment, welfare, health issues are important to Australians — they affect our quality of life — whereas the republic issue does not. When Australia was doing extremely well economically, we never heard anything about a republic from the political parties.

[margin: how are they important?] *[margin: explain]* *[margin: expand]* *[margin: define]*

Australia is a multicultural society of which all Australians are proud. Republicans try to use the very uneducated view that, '. . . it is wrong for new Australians to swear their allegiance to a monarch of another country'. These new Australians must recognise that the monarchy has been a fundamental part of our life for many years; an institution. A true example of how republicans try to direct people into believing in the same cause as they do is highlighted in the paragraph below:

[margin: most (replacing "all")]

> *The Mayor of Coffs Harbour, Counsellor John Smith, was outraged by the new wording of the Citizenship Pledge. He claimed it would lead to charges of treason, treachery and sedition. He declared he would continue to use the old citizenship oath including its references to the Queen. Senator Nick Bolkus, the Minister for immigration, acted decisively and removed Counsellor Smith's right to undertake ceremonials for the conferral of citizenship.*

This shows that the republicans are acting undemocratically, going against the basic principles this country was founded on. They are desperate to express their views without looking at the matter objectively and clearly. Another major point that leads on from the one above is who is behind the republic? Do they have vested interests in Australia becoming a republic? Are they really concerned about Australia or do they want to become King or Queen themselves?

[margin note: example ✓]

In a recent survey conducted by the Ramis Corporation, people were asked, 'Do you want a republic in Australia?' Some 50 per cent of people said yes, compared to a very respectable 41 per cent of people saying no. This just re-affirms the point that not all Australians want a major change to our constitution. With such a small margin of 9 per cent, one could hardly justify that a clear majority want a republic. Such a major constitutional change would need a two to one margin in favour of a republic before initiating a referendum. This is certainly not evident at this stage and probably won't be for quite a while yet. No majority, no republic!

[margin note: example ✓]

In a speech to the Corowa Shire Council, Paul Keating said, '. . . *I am for a republic for what it can deliver — new sense of unity and national pride in which Australians of this and future generations can share*.' What the Prime Minister has really failed to do in the speech is look at the whole picture. He has only talked about the pride and standing Australia will have as a republic. He has raised trivial and minor points for a republic and certainly hasn't looked at the negatives associated with a republic.

[margin note: It is not accurate to say]

~~In summary one can conclude~~ that the republic is not a 'necessary evil'. Why spend so much money on changing the constitution when it could be spent on better things in our community, rather than creating a banana republic. ~~in the first place?~~ Let's hope that in the future an enlightened Australia will still be part of the monarchy, not denying our heritage or past but looking to the future under strong stability governed by the Queen of Australia.

Final draft

REPUBLICANISM WOULD BE GOOD FOR AUSTRALIA
A republic would certainly not be good for Australia! Australia is a new and vibrant country

with a proud past and a well-loved constitutional monarch as its head of state. It has a proud future ahead of itself as part of the British Commonwealth.

The strongest reason for Australia retaining the monarchy is that the monarchy has served us extremely well. It creates stability between the government and its people. It also serves in a figurehead role. We have been part of a monarchy for over 200 years. The monarchy has been tried and proven to be highly successful.

Unfortunately, the republic issue is being turned into a political diversion by the Prime Minister. This diversion is a complete distraction from the main issues we, as Australians, are facing. Environment, welfare and health issues are important to Australians — they affect our quality of life — whereas the republican issue does not. Thus, the republic would not be good for Australia. People want their hospital system working at its best as it may directly affect them — the perceived Australian with 2.3 children does not give a hoot whether the constitution offers hereditary monarchy or a republic. They want to breathe clean air and make sure that there are provisions in place for adequate child care. When Australia was doing well economically, we didn't hear anything about a republic from the government! The republican issue is a pure diversion from the real issues.

Australia is a multicultural society of which most Australians are proud. Republicans try to use the argument that it is wrong for non-British new Australians to swear their allegiance to a monarch of another country. These new Australians must recognise that the monarchy has been a fundamental part of our life for many years; an institution of pride. A true example of how republicans try to force people into believing in the same cause as they do is highlighted in the paragraph below.

The Mayor of Coffs Harbour, Councillor John Smith, was outraged by the new wording of the Citizenship Pledge. He claimed it would lead to charges of treason, treachery and sedition. He declared he would continue to use the old citizenship oath including its references to the

> Queen. Senator Nick Bolkus, the Minister for
> Immigration, acted decisively and removed
> Councillor Smith's right to undertake
> ceremonials for the conferral of citizenship.

This shows that the republicans are acting undemocratically — going against the basic principles on which this country was founded. They are desperate to express their views without looking at the matter objectively and fairly. A republic would do no good, rather it would antagonise people who have fought for King and Country.

Those people arguing for a republic need to take account of our traditions and accepted values. Do they have vested interests in Australia becoming a republic?

In a recent survey conducted by the Ramis Corporation, 600 people were asked, 'Do you want a republic in Australia?' Some 50 per cent of people said 'Yes', compared to a very respectable 41 per cent of people saying 'No'. This just reaffirms the point that not all Australians want a major change to our constitution. With such a small margin of 9 per cent one could hardly claim that a clear majority want a republic. Such a major constitutional change would need a two to one margin in favour of a republic before initiating a referendum. This is certainly not evident at this stage and probably won't be for quite a while yet. No majority, no republic!

In a speech to the Corowa Shire Council, Paul Keating said, 'I am for a republic for what it can deliver — new sense of unity and national pride in which Australians of this and future generations can share . . .' The whole picture has not been considered. The Prime Minister has talked only about the pride and standing Australia would have as a republic. The world would be far more impressed if we were not in debt to overseas interests! He has raised trivial and minor points for a republic and certainly hasn't looked at the negatives associated with a republic. Now, although the Prime Minister has stated he wants Australia to remain part of the Commonwealth, one would wonder what would happen under a new leader? Would we still be part of the Commonwealth? With

> the Queen as our head of state we are a natural member of the influential Commonwealth — an organisation which has a considerable amount of power in international economics and human rights. This is an incredibly vital organisation of which we are part.
>
> Another argument put forth rightly by republicans is that Australia should have an Australian head of state. Effectively, we already do. The Honourable Bill Hayden, Governor General, is an Australian.
>
> It is not accurate to say that the republic is a 'necessary evil'. Why spend so much money on changing the constitution when it could be spent on better things in our community rather than creating a banana republic? Let's hope that in the future an enlightened Australia will still be part of the monarchy, not denying our heritage or past, but looking to the future under strong stability governed by the Queen of Australia. God save the Queen!

2 Construct your own essay plan on one of the topics below.
   Sport should be compulsory in all Australian schools.
   Smoking should be banned in all public places.
   - Be sure to develop a structure that works. One idea must flow naturally into the next. Include in your plan the main point for each paragraph and the evidence that you would include.
   - Use your library to help you locate additional arguments and evidence.
   - Discuss your plan with your teacher or with a friend. Make alterations if necessary.
   - Make a list of key words and phrases appropriate to the essay. Use your thesaurus if you need help.

3 Write your first draft, ensuring that you follow the plan you developed above. You will find that changes occur to you throughout the process of writing. (Use the sample essay drafts above as guides for your own writing). When you have finished your first draft, follow the steps below to come up with your final draft.
   - Have your draft checked by your teacher.
   - Edit the first draft, taking into account any suggestions offered by your teacher.
   - Write the final draft of your essay. The essay should be from 700 to 800 words long.

4 Here are some additional argumentative essay topics that you can choose from to help you polish your techniques.
   Life is worth more than gold.
   Sacrifice our future. Crucify our past.
   'Mothers just don't matter anymore.' Teryl Zarnow

Australia's heritage is multicultural. A British flag is inappropriate.
Gifted children are generally disadvantaged in our education system.
Euthanasia. The only solution.
Abortion. Every woman's right.
Children in single-parent families are disadvantaged.
Children in single-parent families are not disadvantaged.
We can learn more from animals in the wild than we can from ourselves.

- **In argumentative writing you are expected to argue a case objectively by developing a viewpoint and providing supporting evidence.**

- **To create the objective tone required, a formal essay should be written from the third-person point of view ('he', 'she' and 'it'), rather than the first-person point of view ('I').**

- **Argumentative essays should contain an introduction, body paragraphs, a rebuttal (which can be in each paragraph), and a conclusion.**

- **All opinions must be supported with evidence; avoid being emotional; organise your ideas and ensure that the introduction and conclusion fulfil their roles.**

- **Create an effective style by paying attention to the language and sentence structure you use to put your ideas together.**

- **Plan your argumentative essay carefully so that it has clarity and a logical structure.**

- **Be prepared to make at least two drafts of your essay.**

Part Two

Thinking creatively

11

Relatively speaking

Constructing analogies

Drop eggs into a bowl of water and the bad ones swim to the top. So with human beings, the true are more often than not submerged, the specious rise.

Patrick White

Your choice of language influences how effectively you convey messages to your audience. It is important that your audience fully understands the point you wish to make. One way to make sure of this is to compare one thing with another to emphasise your point. For instance, 'The athlete ran like a startled gazelle' compares a human sprinter and a four-legged speedy animal. Similarities between the two, however, exist only on the surface. If you explore further, the comparison breaks down. A sprinter's purpose, stride and speed is in fact totally different from what an animal does naturally — fleeing from something that has frightened it.

When you go beyond simple similarities to use comparisons to make a point, or illustrate an argument, you are using analogies.

Analogies are useful when developing an argument as they can help make a complex point more clearly and simply. As well they can create a visual image which, at times, is more persuasive than the written word.

Time to think

1 Read the quotation from Patrick White at the beginning of this chapter.
- What two things are being compared?
- Explain the meaning of the comparison.
- Describe the similarities and differences between the two things.
- Can you see any problem in the comparison?

How do analogies work?

To help you understand how analogies work and what effects they can create, look carefully at these examples.

1 A thought is an abstract quality. You may expand on it by following the many different aspects that arise from that thought.

> **After a little time the thought took root and grew.**

In other words, a thought can 'grow'. But can it produce roots, as a plant does to draw nourishment from soil or water and produce a structure of stem and leaves?

So the analogy between a thought and a plant is useful in that it conveys an image of how a thought grows. However, the two are quite different in that one is an abstract activity of the human brain, while the other is a material object, which does not possess a brain that directs it.

2 In the following analogy strong images are created. However, it does show that differences in the two things being compared can cause a weakness in the analogy.

> Fire, like a reeling drunk, disdains reason.
>
> (*Time*, 24 January 1994)

A fire and a reeling drunk are being compared here. The similarities between them are that neither uses any reason; both can move in any direction without warning; both can be out of control; and both have the potential for destruction. Some differences between them are that fire has no ability to reason under any circumstances, whereas a drunk's inability to reason is due to a temporary cause; and that one is human and the other is not.

 Time to think

1 Many consider Dr Martin Luther King's public speech on civil rights for American blacks in August 1963 to be the finest political address delivered in the English language. King used the analogy below to challenge the American people. Read the analogy and answer the questions that follow.

> I have a dream that one day this nation will rise up and live out the meaning of its creed . . . that all men are created equal.
>
> I have a dream that one day, even the State of Mississippi, a desert State, sweltering in the heat of injustice and oppression will be transformed into an oasis of freedom and justice.

- What are the two things being compared in this speech?
- What are the similarities between the two things?
- What are the differences between the two things?
- Why was the State of Mississippi a 'desert State' to King? To what, in particular, was he referring?
- Does the analogy work? Explain why or why not.
- What information does King provide to his listeners by using the analogy?
- Do you find the analogy convincing?

Why use analogies?

Analogies can be humorous, shocking, serious, offensive, supportive, critical, gentle or aimed at praising someone. When a writer is presenting a point of view on an issue, analogies can be used to persuade, to illustrate, and to provoke or evoke a reader response.

Time to think

1 Read through these analogies and work out why a writer would use them.
   - A tour of different chocolate shops is like experiencing heaven on earth.
   - Walking to portable classrooms in winter is like taking a trip to Siberia.
   - Looking through a kaleidoscope is like being immersed in a sea of crystals.
   - Students receiving an education in the nineties are simply guinea pigs in an education researcher's cage.
   - Every winter Saturday in Melbourne crowds of people make their weekly pilgrimage to worship the great God football.
   - The effect of drought is like the surrender of the land to a conquering army.
   - Old age is a gift to be enjoyed in private.

2 Here is a list of ten things with which you should be familiar. Select five and create your own analogy around each word or phrase. Remember, you are comparing one thing with another.

telephones	a grandmother
sunscreen	homework
football	a noisy child
music	school
a talkative person	birthdays

3 Read the passage below (*Simply Living*, March 1994). It is an example of how an analogy can be used in a piece of writing.

   > Blake's analogy of parenting being like having a small plant kept under glass, is one to which parents can relate. There comes a time when the protective glass cover must be lifted from the small plant, in order for it to grow. In surviving, the plant's roots grow deep.
   >
   > 'The task of the parent is getting the balance right,' he says with a knowing smile. 'To strain enough to produce growth and not to over strain so it wipes them out. That's the challenge, the difficulty and the excitement of parenthood.'

Using this passage as a model, create your own two-paragraph analogy on the relationship between parents and their children. Look for similarities and differences and see how far you can take the comparison. Remember that you are creating an analogy to either illustrate or clarify the issue.

★ An analogy is a comparison made between two things in order to emphasise a point or illustrate an argument.

★ Analogies are useful when developing an argument as they can create a visual image to help make a complex point clearly and simply.

★ Analogies can add colour to your writing by evoking an image that will provoke a response in your audience.

12

The art of brainstorming

Creative planning

When schemes are laid in advance, it is surprising how often the circumstances fit in with them.

Sir William Ostler

The art of brainstorming

The term brainstorming (or mindmapping) simply means planning before you write. Brainstorming is a creative way of putting your ideas down on paper. Instead of starting with a structured plan, the idea is to allow your thoughts to flow freely from one to the other before organising them into a logical order.

Working up a brainstorm

These steps will help you to create a constructive brainstorm:

- Select a piece of paper — A4 or larger.
- Having selected your issue or topic, write the main (or key) word in the centre of your piece of paper.
- Draw a square, a circle, a cloud, a triangle, or any other shape around the word in the centre.
- Draw branches, or lines, coming out from your shape. Each branch represents a new idea. Along the branches write down in any order all ideas that come to mind.
- Draw secondary branches coming out of your original branches for any ideas that seem connected to ideas on the first branches.
- When you have run out of ideas look over each one and cross out those that do not seem to fit.
- Use different coloured pens or pencils to highlight those ideas that seem to be connected. These will form the basis of your paragraphs.
- You now have a plan for a persuasive piece of writing. It should look something like this.

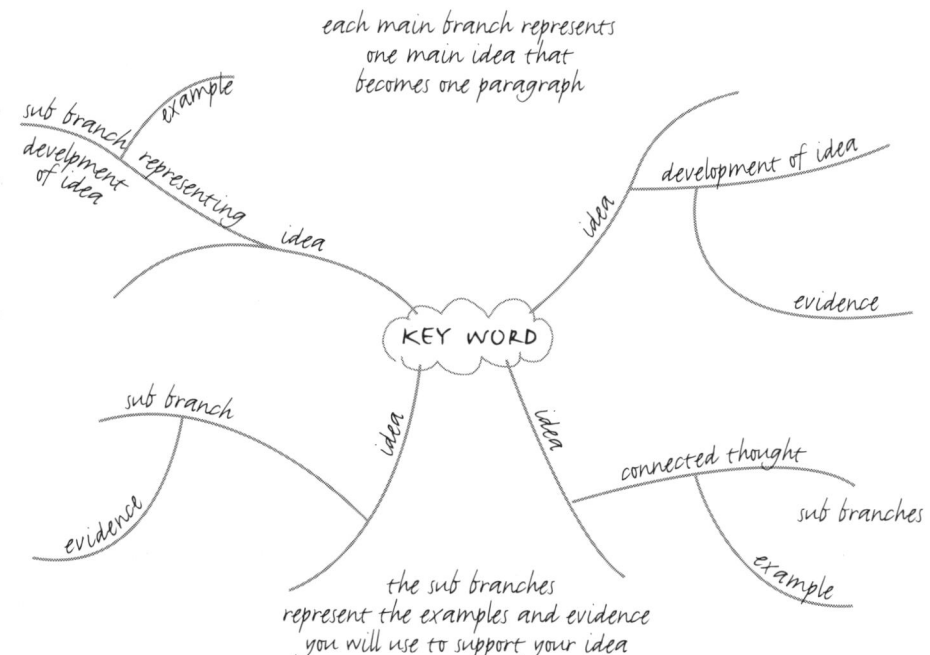

Here is a sample brainstorm on 'The increasing use of computers and video games is creating illiteracy in adolescents'.

COMPUTERS

- Limited story lines therefore limited access to new experiences
- Adolescence — particularly vulnerable time in life. Much questioning of reading for its own sake
- Stereotyping of males and females
- Physical impact on eyes and reading skills
- Define literacy/illiteracy
- Visual images stronger than written word
- Difference between computer literacy and written and oral literacy
- Video games replacing reading as a leisure activity
- Spellcheck versus the dictionary
- Erode ability to think, structure, develop ideas and design presentations
- Easier to press a button than consult a book
- Create laziness
- Loss of imagination
- Handwriting versus the computer printer
- Electronic equipment more limited than the written word
- Too many adolescents attracted to violent video games
- Students no longer practise writing skills. Consider copy book writing of the past. Pen and ink

Time to think

1 Using the above suggestions and examples as a guide, work up a brainstorm on one of the issues below.
   - Teenagers need enormous support within the changing structure of the family.
   - Peer-group pressure on adolescents is destructive.
   - Advertising that emphasises the 'body beautiful' should be banned.
   - The study of Aboriginal culture should be part of Australian secondary education.

★ **It is important to plan before you write to make sure that you examine, consider, use or reject all ideas connected with a topic.**

★ **A brainstorm is a creative approach to planning and allows you to capture ideas as they skip across your mind, before they disappear forever.**

★ **A visual plan of your brainstorm enables you to see easily the connections between ideas.**

★ **The final step in planning is to organise the ideas you wish to include in a logically structured plan.**

13

The image before us

Cartoons and photographs

... identifying ourselves with the visual image of ourselves has become an instinct.

D.H. Lawrence

Cartoons

Most newspapers and magazines contain cartoons. Sometimes they accompany an article, at other times they appear by themselves. A cartoon is a quick and appealing visual way of conveying a point of view. A humorous approach to a serious issue can be an effective way of making a point. Even without humour, a single cartoon can often summarise a complex issue. It is much easier for us to take in a visual message than it is to read and absorb a 500-word essay on the same subject.

Time to think

1 In the cartoon below, Spooner makes a comment on 'Modern Marriage and Divorce'. Look at it carefully and answer the questions that follow.

- On first glance, what seems to be happening in the cartoon?
- When you look more closely, what else do you see is happening?
- What emotions do you think the faces of the people reveal?
- Explain the comment that Spooner is making about modern marriages.

Analysing cartoons

Cartoons contain some, or all, of the following ingredients.

- visual images
- a caption (words at the bottom of the cartoon)
- dialogue (inside bubbles)
- signs or labels
- symbols (an image that represents something else)
- a message, or point of view, on an issue
- contrasting use of light and shade (the use of varying tones, including white, grey and black)

Time to think

Look at Spooner's cartoon, 'The Hangman', on the right and answer the questions below.
- What is the issue being addressed in the cartoon?
- Which of the ingredients outlined above have been included?
- In a sentence or two, explain what you think is Spooner's message. Which part of the image causes you to think this?
- Look at the use of dark and light tones in the cartoon. What is the effect of the black background?
- What is your reaction to this cartoon?

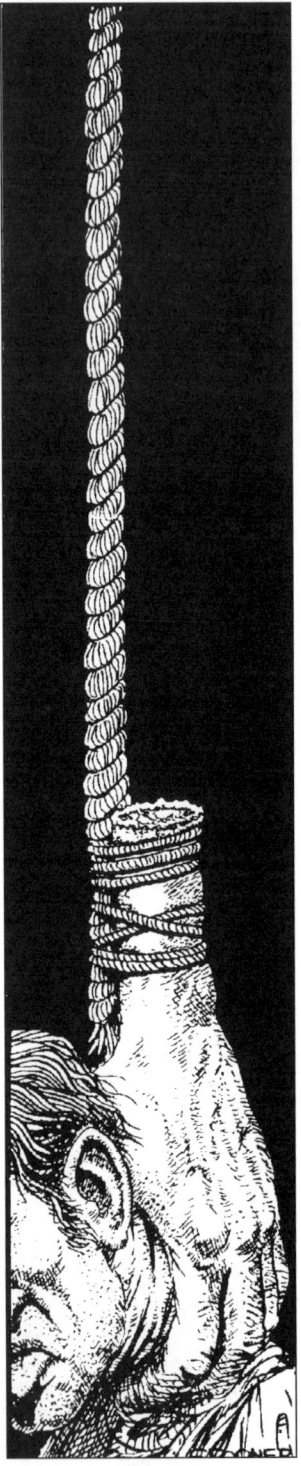

Responding to cartoons

As already mentioned, one purpose of a cartoon is to express a point of view on an issue. In doing so the intention is to generate a response regarding that issue.

Time to think

1 The cartoon, 'Evolution', by Petty (*Age*, 28 December 1993), expresses a view on modern human beings as part of the evolutionary process. Look closely at the cartoon and follow the suggestions below.

Form pairs or groups of three, and nominate one person to write down the points made during your discussion and another to report back to the class on the group's findings. If you have a third person in your group, this person can act as a chairperson by directing the discussion and ensuring that all tasks are completed.
- Discuss the cartoon and write down what you think is Petty's attitude to modern human beings.

- Discuss each of your own views on evolution and record the findings.
- Look carefully at the final image of the evolutionary process. To what extent is this a true representation of modern human beings?
- The cartoon deals with the subject of evolution, but says nothing about an alternative explanation for the existence of the world, which is that God created it in six days. Discuss and record the group's ideas on the 'creation' theory.
- Each group should now report back to the class and the class findings should be recorded.
- Using your own findings and those of the class, write a 500-word piece expressing your view on 'The Great Controversy: Evolution or Creation?'. (See Chapter 10 for help in structuring an argument.)

Photographs

Photographs, even more than cartoons, have an immediacy of impact. The message is received at a glance. Many newspaper editors use images to influence the reading public to buy their product. Have you ever noticed how often the front pages of daily newspapers contain photographs that either shock or appeal to your emotions in some way? Can you recall seeing graphic and colourful representations of accident scenes, or of footballers with blood streaming down their faces? Or appealing and happy pictures of lotto winners, Olympic gold medallists, smiling children, or cute animals?

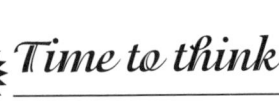

Time to think

1 Discuss the questions below as a class group.
- Do you think newspapers lure readers into purchase by including appealing photographs?
- Do you think newspapers should only provide quality written reports, or are photographs an important part of reporting?
- How would you respond to the following images? What is the purpose of including images such as these in the media? Write down your responses.
    - a small baby lying in a humidicrib
    - a ballerina
    - a young child who appears to have been the victim of a bashing
    - a lone round-the-world yachtsman reaching home
    - a chaotic accident scene with a body lying on the ground
    - an elderly man who has been robbed
    - a small girl displaying all the trophies she has won in baby contests
    - a footballer taking a spectacular mark
    - a person suffering from a disease such as cancer or AIDS

2 Newspapers sometimes construct images to cause a particular effect. Each of the images above has been constructed by the photographer, Albert Comper. Not one of them depicts a real situation. Study them closely and answer the questions below.
- Explain your first reaction to each photograph.
- What emotion is conveyed to the audience in each photograph?
- How do you think each image was constructed?
- Write a caption for each photograph.
- If each of these photographs accompanied an article in a newspaper, what would the issue in the article be?

3 Over the next week, collect the front-page photographs from one daily newspaper. In a couple of sentences, describe your reaction to each one. Bring them to class and swap them with a friend who has used a different newspaper. Compare your reactions. What observations can you make about the types of photographs used by the different newspapers?

★ **Use of visual images is an effective way to communicate a message quickly and clearly.**

★ **Cartoons can deal with serious and complex issues in an appealing and lighthearted way, and can generate strong responses in an audience.**

★ **Photographs are immediate and graphic, and can stimulate emotional reactions in a way that words alone often cannot.**

14

I say this, you say that

Comparing attitudes through songs

Attitudes affect our whole approach to thinking…

Edward de Bono, *Teach Your Child to Think*

94   Thinking creatively

Change occurs as a result of developments and altered needs in our environment. For example, what may be valued in one decade may no longer be valued in the next. Over time, individual and social views and attitudes can vary.

Popular songs have, for many years, been a record of society's changing attitudes or ways of thinking on particular subjects. Songs are an important way of communicating, as they have access to a large range of people. For example, anyone listening to the radio when a song is played is being exposed to someone else's attitude or viewpoint. Song lyrics can present an oral history of the changes occurring in society and of the attitudes towards those changes.

Time to think

1 Below are the lyrics of two songs. The first, *Tar and Cement* by Verdelle Smith, was recorded in the 1960s. The second, *(Nothing But) Flowers* by Talking Heads, was recorded in the 1990s. Both are about progress and change, but the attitudes expressed are different. Read the lyrics of both and answer the questions that follow.

Tar and Cement

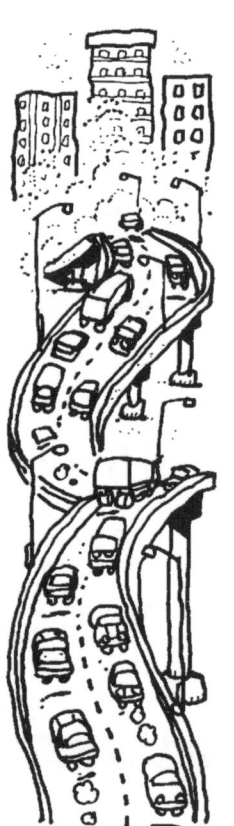

*The town I came from was quiet and small,
we played in the meadows, where the grass grows so tall.
In summer the lilacs would grow ev'rywhere,
the laughter of children would float in the air.*

*As I grew older, I had to roam,
far from my fam'ly, far from my home,
Into the city where lives can be spent
lost in the shadows of tar and cement.*

*and ev'ry night I'd sit alone and learn
what loneliness meant
Up in my rented room above a world
Of tar and cement.*

*Each day I'd wake up, look at the sky,
think of the meadows where I used to lie,
Then I'd remember, all of that's gone,
you're in the city, better rush on,*

*Get what you came for before it's too late,
get what you came for, the meadows can wait.*

*So every night I'd sit alone and learn
what loneliness meant.*

I say this, you say that

*Up in my rented room above a world
of tar and cement.*

*Many years later, tired at last,
I headed for home to look for my past,
I looked for the meadows, there wasn't a trace,
six lanes of highway had taken their place.*

*Where were the lilacs and all that they meant?
Nothing but acres of tar and cement
Yet I can see it there so clearly now
Where has it gone?
Yes I can see it there so clearly now,
Where has it gone?*

*Where are the meadows?
Tar and cement.
Where are the lilacs?
Tar and cement.
Where is the tall grass?
Tar and cement.
The laughter of children?
Tar and cement.
Nothing but acres
Tar and cement.
Acres and acres
Tar and cement.*

- On your first reading of the title, what did you think the song would be about?
- When this song was popular, the growth of cities and highways was extremely rapid and country areas were being overtaken by this growth. What is the comparison being made in the first two verses?
- What has been 'lost' in this song? Which lines in particular convey that sense of loss?
- What attitudes does the person in the song have towards the country before and after she leaves?
- Consider the words, 'What loneliness meant'. What attitude do they express towards the city? What features of the city have caused this response?
- Why would *Tar and Cement* have been a popular song in the 1960s?
- What is the overall attitude towards progress in this song?

(Nothing but) Flowers

*Here we stand
Like an Adam and an Eve
Waterfalls
The Garden of Eden*

*Two fools in love
So beautiful and strong
The birds in the trees
Are smiling upon them
From the age of the dinosaurs
Cars have run on gasoline
Where, where have they gone?
Now, it's nothing but flowers.
There was a factory
Now there are mountains and rivers.
You got it, you got it
We caught a rattlesnake
Now we got something for dinner.
We got it, we got it
There was a shopping mall
Now it's all covered with flowers
You've got it, You've got it
If this is paradise
I wish I had a lawn mower
You've got it, we've got it.
Years ago
I was an angry young man
I'd pretend
That I was a billboard
Standing tall
By the side of the road
I fell in love
With a beautiful highway.
This used to be real estate
Now it's only fields and trees
Where, where is the town?
Now, it's nothing but flowers
The highways and cars
Were sacrificed for agriculture
I thought that we'd start over
But I guess I was wrong
Once there were parking lots
Now it's a peaceful oasis
You've got it. You've got it.
This was a Pizza Hut
Now it's all covered with daisies
You got it, you got it.
I miss the Honky Tonks,
Dairy Queens and 7-Elevens
You got it, you got it.*

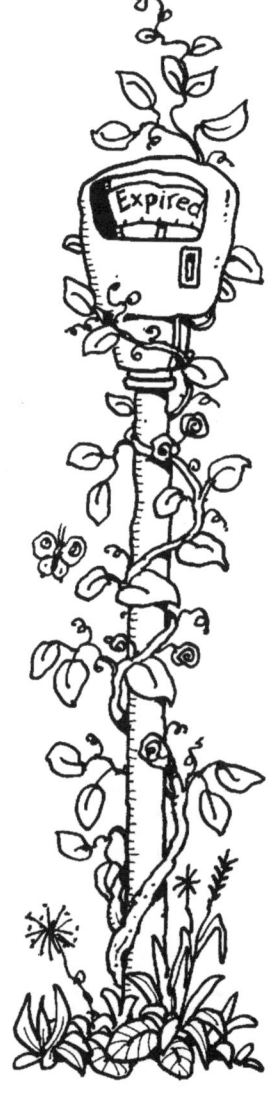

And as things fell apart
Nobody paid much attention
You got it, you got it.
I dream of cherry pies
Candy bars and chocolate chip cookies.
You got it, you got it
We used to microwave
Now we just eat nuts and berries
You got it, you got it
This was a discount store,
Now it's turned into a cornfield
You got it, you got it
Don't leave me stranded here,
I can't get used to this lifestyle

- Find a line in this song that hints at people's lack of awareness of the effects of events happening around them.
- The person in this song seems to yearn for the problems of city life. Is this really the case, or is the person suggesting that our modern lifestyle has gone so far that reverting to nature would be impossible for us? Explain your response.
- Most people would recognise the names Pizza Hut, Dairy Queen and Seven Eleven, so these references do not have to be explained in the song. What does this say about advertising and its ability to plant words into our vocabulary? What are some other examples of brand names that have become automatically recognisable to us? Do you think we have a consumer approach to life?
- Consider the words, 'If this is paradise, I wish I had a lawnmower'. What attitude is conveyed in this line?
- The lines, 'The highways and cars/Were sacrificed for agriculture' and 'Once there were parking lots/Now it's a peaceful oasis', express the opposite view of many people. What other lines express a view that is opposite to your own? Do you think that this method of expression gives more impact to the lyrics?
- Describe the songwriter's attitude towards progress.

2 To help you see how individuals' and society's ways of thinking can change over time, it might be useful to compare the attitudes on 'progress' expressed in the lyrics of the two songs above.
- How do the lyrics, written 25 years apart, indicate the changes in what is regarded as valuable?
- What has shaped the attitudes of the people in each song?
- Do you think the songs would have an impact on the attitudes of an audience? Explain why or why not, using lines from each song to illustrate your points.
- Have a look at the titles of each song. Why do you think each title has been chosen? Do you think they are the most appropriate titles?

3 Think about your own environment. Do you live in bushland? Are you surrounded by advertising slogans and billboards? Can you hear the traffic from your

bedroom, even with the windows closed? Write your own song expressing your attitude towards changes that are occurring in your environment, or in some part of Australia. Choose language that will persuade people to think about their attitudes.

4 Create either a series of drawings or a photomontage of the changes that you have noticed in an environment familiar to you.

5 Write a letter to a very close friend describing your reactions to either of the environments described in the two songs above.

- ★ The views of individuals and societies can alter over time as a result of changes that occur in the environment and culture.
- ★ Over the years, popular songs have recorded the changes in society's attitudes towards many issues.
- ★ Songs are an important tool of communication because they are accessible to a wide range of people and their impact can be far-reaching.

15

Thinking creatively

A pathway to effective thinking

> *Every valuable creative idea must always be logical in hindsight.*
>
> **Edward de Bono,** *Teach Your Child to Think*

So far in this book you have discovered all the processes necessary to achieve a clear, structured piece of writing or a precise and interesting speech. Think of how much more effective and vibrant your writing can become when you add a creative thinking approach to these processes.

Edward de Bono, a leader in creative-thinking programs, says in his book *Six Thinking Hats*, that when we imagine ourselves wearing hats of different colours for different ways of thinking we can improve our thinking effectiveness. When given a problem to solve, or a tricky decision to make, de Bono suggests that if we imagine ourselves putting on a particular coloured 'thinking hat' our creative thought processes become clearer. It is similar to the idea expressed when a primary school teacher asks students to put on their 'thinking caps'. This deliberate imaginary action can change your way of thinking. Edward de Bono says:

> The purpose of the six thinking hats is to unscramble thinking so that a thinker is able to use one thinking mode at a time — instead of trying to do everything at once. The best analogy is that of color printing. Each color is printed separately and in the end they all come together.

De Bono's six different-coloured hats are white, red, black, yellow, green and blue. The style of thinking related to each different colour is set out below.

WHITE	pure facts, figures and information, objective approaches, disciplined, direct, neutral
RED	acknowledges emotions and feelings, hunches and intuition as part of thinking
BLACK	negative judgement, why something will not work, indicating faults objectively
YELLOW	brightness and optimism, positive outlooks, constructive approaches, seeing opportunities
GREEN	creative ideas, room for growth and development, moving forward to see and allow for new ideas
BLUE	control of a situation, organising and structuring, providing definition and focus

Time to think

1 Listed below is a range of thinking situations. Match each one with the appropriately coloured hat.
   - There will come a day when we will no longer use money. All transactions will be made with credit cards. You won't even be able to pay for a stamp with money. Big Brother will really be watching then!
   - The solution to the problem of cleaning gutters is to make them detachable. No more spouting clogged by gum leaves because you're scared of heights and can't climb up on the roof. Just detach the gutter from the roof by removing detachable brackets and your problems are solved.
   - The market in emu farming is expanding. It looks small now, but the investment possibilities are there. People want to be able to see where their money is going, and it is supporting an animal native to Australia.
   - It was a beautiful house, but the price — $345 000 — was too high. We decided to buy the one for $250 000. This means that we can do about $10 000 worth of landscaping.
   - I have a feeling that Mum's going to give me a kitten for my birthday.
   - The most efficient way of organising this disco and ensuring that it works is to give everyone at this meeting a job to do. In that way we will know that everything will be done properly.

2 Now for a thinking game. You will need a team of six people. Each person represents a different-coloured hat and takes on a different role within the team. Imagine yourself placing your particular coloured hat on your head each time you speak and write within the limits of your role. It can be fun to make and wear your coloured hat throughout the game.
   - Your team has been asked to design a multi-million dollar advertising campaign for a new drink, SCHWEPPSI. It is a drink for the younger generation, but the company wants the older generation to buy it as well. You will need television promotion, jingles for radio, billboards across the country, budget management, and visions for the future to ensure that the campaign will last.
   - The six people brought in to assist with this lucrative campaign are:

   White hat thinking   The accountant, who provides the financial detail: costs of the campaign, cost of the product, and so on.

   Red hat thinking   A person who can explain the type of 'feelings' involved in purchasing a drink and knows how to present the emotions on television.

   Black hat thinking   A person who can see the problems that might arise with the campaign and can express them clearly and calmly.

   Yellow hat thinking   A person who represents the soft-drink company and who can see the market potential and opportunities for the product.

Green hat thinking   A person with creative talent who has many ideas, can see the room for growth and expansion in the marketplace, and can draw the images that will be required for television and for billboards.

Blue hat thinking   A person who can bring the team together, prepare a timeline, direct all members of the group on their involvement, and ensure that everyone knows the target audience and the objectives.

- Your first meeting takes place in the company boardroom. This is the procedure to follow:

  Step 1   The six members of the group have a preliminary discussion. In this meeting each person is given a role according to the six hats process of thinking. Each person outlines his or her views on the product and the campaign.

  Step 2   Each person writes down his or her ideas, using the definitions of the coloured hats above as a guideline.

  Step 3   The group comes back together to discuss proposals and finalise details.

  Step 4   The proposal is submitted to the soft-drink company.

Your presentation must be clear, organised, straightforward, and visually pleasing. Here are some guidelines on areas to cover:

Name of product
Aims and objectives
The market/who will buy the product?
Visual images
Slogans/jingles
Rationale for the campaign
Extent of the campaign
Competition in the market
Cost of the campaign

3 Has your thinking changed after using the six hats approach? How effective are the different-coloured hats in making you aware of how you are thinking? Do the hats help you to change the way you tackle a problem?

★ **Thinking in a creative way can improve your thinking effectiveness.**

★ **Edward de Bono's 'six hats' approach to thinking, which involves the deliberate imaginary action of wearing different-coloured hats for different thought processes, can change your way of thinking.**

16

Gentle persuasion

Language of influence

All of us who use the mass media are the shapers of society...

Bill Berrnbach

Everyone at some time uses tactics, deliberately or not, to influence another person or group of people. The techniques used to persuade often depend on experience, knowledge of the person or group being persuaded, and the subject of persuasion. For example, a young child in a supermarket might ask a parent for a chocolate bar over and over again until the parent gives up, in sheer frustration, and the chocolate bar is bought. The child has been successful. The parent has been persuaded.

The world of advertising survives by using methods of persuasion to influence particular groups in society. The people who design advertisements work on all the emotions and all the problems that people might have, to persuade them to buy a particular product. In many ways this strategy is not too different from the one undertaken by the child in the supermarket.

Analysing advertisements

If you look around, you will see many instances of advertisers' use of the not-so-gentle art of persuasion. The examples below clearly show how advertisements can target the emotions and expectations of their audience in an attempt to influence their behaviour.

- An advertisement for a cleaning product uses the image of a baby crawling around on a kitchen floor, accompanied by the words, 'You want to give them the best'. This obviously attempts to appeal to parents' desire to protect their family and to provide all that is 'best'. Even better if the price is lower. This means that the 'best' can be provided while money is saved. This appeals to the 'hip-pocket nerve' and the all important need to economise.
- Teenagers can be vulnerable in the hands of advertisers. Any collectable items, such as basketball and football cards, provide a seemingly endless drain on many teenagers' hard-won pocket money or pay. If these collectables can be advertised at prices even slightly cheaper than usual they will sell much more easily and quickly. The advertiser is appealing to teenagers' sense of competition, awareness of money, and consciousness of peer-group pressure.
- 'Are you tired? Rundown? Need a break?' Colourful images of a tropical island stare out at you, enticing you as you enthusiastically nod 'yes' to all these questions. 'The great escape.' That's for me. You rush off and book your tickets. You have been persuaded. Your desire to relax, to be free of the rush and hurry of life, has been targetted by the advertiser, who knows that some part of you will respond to this need to get away.

Listed below is a range of possible emotions, weaknesses, problems or needs to which advertisers might appeal:

fear	jealousy	death	hostility
love	envy	pain	beauty
hate	grief	time	vanity
anger	money	illness	family
success	age	professionalism	health
happiness	humour	war	food

Other areas of appeal could include:

a need to belong   a wish to be elegant
a search for identity   a desire to be independent

a desire to be one of the crowd
a desire to get ahead in life
a need for self-reliance
a need for status

a desire to feel good
a link to tradition
a need to have information
a wish to protect family

The approach of advertisers can be expressed as simply as follows:

STARTING POINT   Each group in society has its weaknesses and deep-seated emotional needs.

INTENTION   If people buy our products they will be provided with a soothing solution to their problems or needs.

Time to think

1 Analyse the slogans below and identify the emotions, needs or attitudes being appealed to in each.
   - Slow down. Live longer.
   - You will never be stranded again. The portable phone . . . just for you.
   - Collect your bonus pack! Free with any purchase!
   - Yoghurt. Nutritionally superior.
   - The legend in the jeans.
   - Used by generations of women. The perfect nourishment for your skin!
   - The exercise tape to suit your needs. You can use it when no one is watching.
   - The drink of men . . . and women.
   - For your pet. If you care.
   - Education for success.

2 Think of five television, newspaper or magazine advertisements you have seen. From the lists above decide what appeals the advertiser has used in them.

3 Consider the advertisement on page 106 and the handwritten notes on page 107 and answer the questions below. The handwritten notes analyse how the advertisement has been designed to appeal to an audience.
   - At what audience is the advertisement aimed?
   - Whose opinion is being expressed in the advertisement? How do you know?
   - In the top photograph there are some images that represent success. What are they?
   - Examine the visual imagery and the dialogue, then describe the impression you are given of the relationship between the father and son.
   - List all of the problems that the advertisement claims will be solved if the product is purchased.
   - Find the words that have been repeated in the advertisement. Why do you think they have been repeated?
   - One aim of advertisers is to link a positive point of view to emotions. Has this occurred in this advertisement?
   - Write down all the types of appeal at work in this advertisement.
   - Do you think the audience would be persuaded to buy the packages? Explain your response.

Thinking creatively

" I don't want to think twice about computers. I just want everything we do to look great."

What you really want from a computer.

" Sure I'm still working, but I'm also around a lot more."

What you need.

Whatever you want from a computer, Microsoft's new Home and Office Packs make sure you get it in a single, intelligent, easy to use package.

The Home Pack gives you a matched set of fully compatible Microsoft® programs. Microsoft Works lets you write letters, balance the family budget, keep records, make charts and even illustrate. Creative Writer lets you and your family put ideas into fun words and pictures. While Entertainment Pack is brimming with fantastic games.

The Office Pack gives you all the business software you need in today's competitive world. Microsoft Office Professional lets you write professional letters, analyse your accounts, keep track of your customers, create fantastic presentations, communicate quickly and easily with your colleagues. Microsoft Publisher lets you make interesting newsletters or turn the most complicated document into a breeze. While Microsoft Money lets you keep track of all your personal finances.

Both packs also come with the Microsoft Service Guarantee. So you're only a phone call away from all the assistance you'll need (valid till September 30, 1994).

Whichever pack you choose, Microsoft now gives you what you really want at a price that means you can have it now.

Microsoft **HOME PACK** $229*

Microsoft **OFFICE PACK** $875*

*Promotional Recommended Retail Price.

From now until July 31, 1994, you can buy the new Microsoft Home and Office Packs at these spectacular promotional prices.

For any further information visit your nearest computer retailer or phone **008 621 622**.

Microsoft®
Making it easier

Frontline Q4GW/G

① Whole frame suggests professionalism and success. If you look good you feel good — image created.

② Dialogue supports visual image. Suggests also a need for computers to support a lifestyle.

③ Father/son image contrasts with busy businesswoman image. Subtle suggestions of role reversal of males and females. Clearly aimed to connect with changing attitudes in society. Strong sense of the 'family' — togetherness. Has emotional impact.

④ Dialogue relates to a problem of modern society by suggesting that by saving time the computer allows people to have more time with their families.

⑤ Use of 'you' throughout the text (or copy) creates a sense of familiarity. The advertisement is talking directly to 'you', and 'you' are drawn in.

⑥ We all have 'wants'. We all have 'needs'. The language suggests the company's awareness of this and stresses the ability of their product to cater for them. This establishes a contrast between people, which is echoed in the photographic material.

⑦ This is what people want; and this language appeals to a need to have less complication in life. This is echoed in the photographs.

⑧ Suggests ability to cater for all people, with emphasis on the 'family'.

⑨ This will satisfy the kids and relieve the parents. Clearly an emotional appeal.

⑩ This is the business paragraph. This information is deliberately placed second. It contrasts with the order established in the photographic material.

⑪ Reassuring. We all want to know that we are not on our own.

⑫ Money. The copy acknowledges and appeals to a basic human desire to have things now. This says that you can have what you want, over and above what you need. An appeal to greed?

The vital information — cost — is supplied clearly. Potential buyers want this information up front. Hidden prices create a lack of trust.

⑬ Here is the trap, designed to make you buy now. The price is 'promotional' and only available for a limited time. The prices are 'spectacular' — this language assumes that 'you must agree'.

⑭ The large print makes the brand name clear. The slogan makes a direct appeal to our desire to simplify our complicated lifestyles.

⑮ Alliteration.

108 Thinking creatively

4 Collect six different advertisements from daily newspapers or magazines. Analyse each, using the above analysis of the Microsoft advertisement as a guide. State clearly the types of appeals used in each and the audience to whom each is directed.

Slogans rule, ok?

Slogans are used by advertisers to grab the attention of the audience. They should be short, sharp and able to be recalled easily.

Time to think

1 Read each of the slogans below answer the questions that follow.

Excellence in hand made glassware
(Krosno glassware, *New Woman*)

YOU COME TO EXPECT A BIT OF SERVE AND VOLLEY IN YOUR BUSINESS DAY
(Burswood Resort Hotel, *Time Australia*)

Food loves Flora
(Flora Herb and Garlic, *Better Homes and Gardens*)

Feel safe, feel confident
(Toyota Camry, *New Woman*)

- At whom is each slogan directed?
- To what emotions, needs, problems or weaknesses do they appeal?
- What do you notice about the lettering used in each advertisement?
- Can you see a relationship between the slogan and the magazine in which it appeared?
- List three other magazines that could feature each slogan?
- Here is a list of six products. Write your own advertisement for each and state the audience and the particular emotion, need, problem or weakness to which an appeal is made.
    unleaded petrol
    mobile phone

woman's magazine
bath soap
breakfast cereal
sports shoes

The language of influence

There is a range of devices available to you when you are writing persuasively. If used carefully, they can help you to create strong, effective writing and assist you to persuade your audience to believe in your point of view.

Rhetorical question
This is a question that is asked not to gain information but to produce an effect. The answer to a rhetorical question is usually implied within it. For example 'There is a rational side to this car, but who cares?' (Holden Calibra, *Time Australia*)

Providing expert information
Quoting information from people who are experts on a subject. Having some knowledge of a subject does not make a person an expert on that subject. For example, if you were writing on the subject of available support services for blind students in schools, an integration officer at the Victorian Institute for the Blind would be an expert on the subject. A cleaner at the Institute would not.

Repetition
Writers often repeat words and phrases to emphasise the point they are making. Repetition creates a rhythm of sound.

> For man holds in his mortal hands the power to abolish all forms of human poverty and all forms of human life.
>
> **John F. Kennedy**

Alliteration
This occurs when the first letter is repeated in words that follow one another. For example:

> **Schoolboy football, the sport of horn-hooting, post-adolescent adults and teenagers trying to terrify the opponent with tangled tactics, fearless flights and marvellous marks.**

Statistics
Statistics are useful when you need factual details to support a point of view expressed. However, before you use them, ensure that they are accurate. Check the source (who compiled them and how they were collected). If they are the result of a survey, it needs to be a recent one. For example, there is no point quoting statistics on marriage and divorce for today if they were compiled in 1955. Also, make sure that the sample used was large enough or wide-ranging enough to be believable. For

example, observations on the number of whales in Australian waters can only be made on Australia-wide figures, not on figures collected in one State only. Finally, check that the figures have not been misinterpreted. For example, a reported ten per cent rise in the rate of teenage suicide could be due to increased reporting or better methods of data collection, rather than an actual increase.

Tone

This is a quality, a feeling, a mood or an effect created by a particular sound in a piece of writing. It relates to the emotions appealed to in a piece of writing, but goes a little further. Tone is influenced by things such as humility, despair, loss, nostalgia, patriotism, flamboyance, sympathy, sadness, empathy, sexuality and positivity. (Use your dictionary to help you find the meanings of any words that you are not familiar with.) For example,

Nostalgia   Are we to forget our ancestors, our inheritance, as we plummet down the road towards republicanism?

Sadness, sympathy   The sight of tiny monkeys, their eyes ablaze with the innocence of their species, is enough to turn the hardest of hearts towards rescuing them from the hands of vivisectionists.

Time to think

1 Write your own example of each of the devices outlined above.
2 Read 'Fighting Fires with Rhetoric' (*Simply Living,* March 1994) and answer the questions that follow.

Fighting Fires With Rhetoric

By JAMIE BROWN, American-born, Australian-based journalist

It is tiresome to find that green bashing has re-emerged to become the latest blood-sport in Australian politics, following the massive New South Wales bush fires in January. And it is annoying to witness talented journalists in the mainstream media refusing to offer their audience an alternative view. Or is it ignorance?

While the fires burned, and volunteers risked their lives to stop them, conservative Members of Parliament and forestry lobbyists were targeting the National Parks and Wildlife Service, along with the entire environmental movement, as being responsible for the destruction. Their reasoning was based on the shaky assumption that traditional hazard reduction burning had been sacrificed in recent years to retain natural bush. While

(continued)

such a situation may apply to some small reserves in and around the leafy northern suburbs of Sydney, the opposite is happening in most rural areas.

The claims that national parks, and wilderness areas especially, are strongholds for bush fires are ludicrous in light of the true facts. While these facts were offered up to the media at the onset by the National Parks and Wildlife Service, the Wilderness Society and the Australian Conservation Foundation, they were rarely given the light of day.

Of the 207 fires that raged through 600 000 hectares of bushland in New South Wales over three weeks in January, only one quarter were alight in national parks, and just three minor blazes were reported in wilderness areas, burning out a total of 240 000 hectares.

There were five times as many fires coming into parks from neighbouring properties as there were fires escaping park boundaries. In addition, the parks service was responsible for 40 per cent of all the state's backburning work in the months leading up to the fires. Yet it controls only five per cent of the state's land area. And, the service has doubled its hazard reduction burning operations over the last decade. Hopefully commonsense will prevail over political point scoring in the findings of a commission of inquiry into the fires.

January's bush fires may be the worst in NSW's history, but taken in isolation they are not the tragedy they seem to be. True, 98 per cent of the country's oldest park, the Royal National Park, has been scorched by intense fire and the only way native animals will recolonise this park – isolated by highway, rivers and ocean – is with some help from humans. However, Royal is an exception. National Parks and Wildlife Service researchers Mark Saxon and Tony Auld point out that Australia's fauna and flora have evolved to survive and even proliferate after severe fire. Where the real damage occurs is after wildlife runs rampant through the landscape for a second time, or third, or fourth time in the ensuing decade.

Many advocates of frequent hazard reduction burning state the practise is environmentally correct because the Aborigines used it. Yes, some tribes used 'firestick farming' to increase biological productivity, and did so for thousands of years. But they did not do it like it is practised today. Once again, the real facts have been lost in the hype.

Dr Peter Kershaw of Monash University's Department of Geography and Environmental Science, says his research into Australia's fire history shows a marked increase in the frequency of bush fires after European settlement. 'This has had a big influence,' he says. 'In Victoria the net result has been a decrease by 50 per cent in rainforest cover.'

Eucalypts, or gum trees, on the other hand have thrived. Kershaw says eucalypts need fire to gain a competitive advantage over other vegetation. As a result they propagate fires themselves – through the oil in their leaves. 'More eucalypts equal more intense fires which are more hazardous to people and plants,' he says.

Frequent fires also reduce diversity. Many Australian plants like wattles and banksia, need to germinate. But these same species need several years between fires before they mature enough to reproduce.

Animals, too, require a delicate balance to survive in the Australian bush. The rare ground parrot, for example, needs constant heath land that has been untouched by fire for at least three years. However, heath unburnt for ten years begins to loose [sic] its attraction for the species.

Taken to the extreme, private reserves in the leafy suburbs of Sydney have not been burned for upward of 40 years. In these places diversity has actually declined because fire – so necessary to the propagation of many native plants – has unnaturally been excluded.

What this sort of evidence points to is the need for smart and specific fire management programs. In Western Australia the implementation of precision burns are starting to make a positive impact on the landscape. In central Australia local Aborigines are working with the CSIRO to develop appropriate 'firestick' management of desert ecosystems. However, on the NSW coast, where firestick farming was not practised in the same way, more research is needed to develop the best

(continued)

fire management tool possible.

'We need to look at details,' says Dr Marilyn Fox, of the University of NSW's geography department. 'In the Royal National Park alone there are several different ecosystems and we need to apply appropriate management for each of them.'

Now is the time to manage our bush as if it really mattered.

- Identify the following devices in the above article: a rhetorical question; use of experts; repetition; alliteration; statistics.
- Are the statistics used believable? Explain why.
- What appeals to emotions, needs and problems are made within the article?
- Describe the author's tone. What words and phrases create this tone?
- What is the main point of the article?
- Do you find the article persuasive? Has it persuaded you? Give your reasons.

3 Write a dialogue between two people on one of the issues below. One person is for the contention, the other is against it. Be sure to use some of the techniques of persuasion outlined above.

There are more lies than truth in advertising.

Advertising is good for us.

The world of advertising is the most persuasive force in all age groups.

- ★ The techniques you use to persuade others depend upon your own experience, your knowledge of the people you are trying to influence, and the issue involved.
- ★ The advertising industry uses many different methods of persuasion to target the emotions and expectations of the audience in an attempt to influence behaviour.
- ★ Slogans are an important persuasive tool of advertisers because they are short, sharp and easy to recall.
- ★ The devices of language that are used to create an impact and persuade an audience include rhetorical questions, providing expert information, repetition, alliteration, use of statistics, and development of an appropriate tone.

17

The learned opposition is...

Debating techniques

Be not rash with thy mouth, and let not thine heart be hasty to utter anything...

Ecclesiastes 5,2

A debate is a test of your oral skills, your knowledge, and your wit. In debating you are not necessarily arguing for a viewpoint that you support. Don't let this concern you. A debate is not an assessment of your beliefs, rather, it is an assessment of your skills.

One objective in debating is to present a case to an audience and to persuade that audience to believe your point of view rather than the opposition's. Another objective is to listen carefully to the opposition's arguments and respond to them in a way that demolishes their case.

The great debate

The participants involved in a formal debate include:
- three speakers on the affirmative (*for* the subject) team
- three speakers on the negative (*against* the subject) team
- chairperson
- adjudicator (the judge or assessor)
- timekeeper

THE SPEAKERS' ROLES

First Speaker
- To introduce the team's case and to present clearly the team's main line of argument. In its preparation the team must have decided on a theme to follow. Each member will speak in support of this approach to the issue.
- To outline briefly the 'angle' to be pursued by the rest of the team.
- To provide accurate definitions of terminology and the topic. While the dictionary is the best place to start for straight definitions, when delivering definitions to the audience, it is more interesting to link them to the direction of the case to be presented. To pursue a lengthy, definition-based approach can be laborious and tedious. Definitions should only be used to clarify terminology.
- To establish the introductory argument in a strong, convincing and positive manner. The argument should grab the audience's attention. The language used should have impact.
- To summarise by referring back to the team's overall approach and to set up for a win.

Second Speaker
- To clear up any problems related to definitions and to emphasise the team's approach.
- To present a rebuttal to the arguments of the opposition's first speaker. It is important to undermine the arguments presented, rather than discrediting the examples.
- To introduce the major arguments and to support them with relevant evidence such as quotations, interesting examples and references to authorities on the subject.
- To emphasise the arguments by summarising them and leaving the way clear for the final speaker.

Third Speaker
- To present a rebuttal to the arguments of the opposition's second speaker. This should be strong, with the underlying aim of showing faults, inconsistencies and irrelevancies in the arguments and thereby demolishing the opposition's case. Remember, you should not be trying to destroy the people on the opposing team.
- To summarise the team's arguments and to show the audience the team's superiority in content and argument.
- To make an effective conclusion. This is the third speaker's main role, so attention should be given to language and delivery. You want the audience to listen to you and to have a lasting, strong impression of you. The third speaker can present new material, but it should be kept to a minimum.

THE CHAIRPERSON'S ROLE
- To welcome the audience.
- To introduce the subject and the teams.
- To direct the speakers to present their arguments at the appropriate time.
- To ask for questions from either side when presentation of cases is complete.
- To ask for questions from the audience, if appropriate.
- To close the debate.

THE ADJUDICATOR'S ROLE
- To assess both teams. Scores are applied on the following scale:
    MATTER = 40 points
    MANNER = 40 points
    METHOD = 20 points
    (See definitions below.)
    TOTAL = 100 points

THE TIMEKEEPER'S ROLE
- To keep the time and to alert each speaker when time has run out. This is usually done by ringing a bell, as a warning, one minute before the time is up, then ringing it again when the time has run out.
- Usually each speaker in a debate has ten minutes to present a case, but this varies according to the circumstance. In a ten-minute speech, no more than three minutes should be spent introducing and setting up the case; one to two minutes on a rebuttal; and the rest of the time given to the delivery of the team's case. As the final impact of each speech lies in the conclusion, at least one minute is appropriate.

May the best team win

As mentioned above, the adjudicator in a formal debate assesses the performance of each team in three areas — matter, manner and method — and applies scores accordingly.

MATTER
Matter (or content) refers to the collection of material on a subject and the appropriate selection from that material to build a clear and concise argument. Matter is the

substance of your argument and includes your definitions, the results of discussions presented, and research completed. All arguments presented in support of your case must be supported by evidence, including statistical information, direct quotations from experts on the subject, analogies, and reasonable conclusions reached from observations made.

The arguments presented by each speaker must be relevant to the stance proposed by the team. If they are not, the case becomes weak.

MANNER

Manner refers to the way you appeal to and the impact you have on the audience. This includes body language, such as hand gestures, body stance, and eye contact with the audience. For example, if you hold your hands stiffly by your sides you will appear nervous and unconfident of your argument. If you start rocking back and forth on your feet, you will distract the audience from your argument. If you constantly look down at your shoes, you will not be communicating with the audience effectively. It is also important, when seated, that you strike a balance between a casual appearance and rigid formality.

The volume and tone of your voice is also important for the assessment of manner. If you are too loud, the audience might not be able to think of anything but ear plugs. If you are too soft, no one will be able to hear you. So, strike a medium volume and keep your audience listening. A well-modulated voice will help to maintain audience interest, while a monotonous one, with no variation, will probably put your listeners to sleep.

Even though you are nervous, it is essential that the audience sees you as confident, but be careful not to be over-confident. A calm assurance, which allows you to sound convincing and persuasive, is the most effective approach.

It is also important that, rather than reading directly from a prepared speech, you talk from notes on small cards. This enables you to rearrange points and insert new ones while the debate is in progress. If, however, you are too dependent on the cards, you will limit your eye contact with the audience. This is a speech. You must remember to talk to the audience.

METHOD

Method refers to your team's organisational skills. It involves the overall structure of the team's approach and the individual organisation of speeches. The arguments must flow logically from one to another, and all three speakers must fulfil their appropriate roles in the debate.

Method also includes ensuring that the audience is informed about the direction of the debate and the definitions within it. In addition, demonstrating that you have a team approach and are committed to your case must be considered in your delivery.

A debate cannot function properly without careful timing. Running out of time, or having time left over, indicates poor organisation skills. Time your speeches before the final delivery. This will assist you with structuring your case and knowing your direction.

Getting ready

It is important to prepare carefully for a debate so that you can present a strong, confident and convincing case. Here are some pointers that will help lay the foundations for a successful debate.

- To prevent any good ideas from escaping, do a quick brainstorm on your topic. Write down in random order any words and phrases connected with the topic that spring to mind (see Chapter 12).
- Be confident, or at least appear to be confident, despite any nervousness.
- Be prepared to speak with strength and have the courage of your convictions.
- Use concise speech — avoid 'ums' and 'ahs'.
- Remember that debating involves teamwork.
- Be prepared to listen carefully to the arguments of the other team.
- Think about how you will express your views effectively.
- Think about your presentation. How do you look? Is your body language direct and confident? Do you have any quirky characteristics?
- Number the cards you refer to in your speech so that you can easily locate a certain point and you do not have loose pages dropping around you.
- Be sure that your team works co-operatively to devise an approach, research the subject (if appropriate), establish roles, and develop arguments.
- Communicate with your other team members during the debate. Passing notes to one another is acceptable, but be wary of talking as this can be very disruptive.
- Remember to make notes on points made by the opposition so you can respond to them in your rebuttal, or during question time.
- Ensure that each team member is aware of the roles of all other participants in the debate.
- Defend your case by condemning the opposition's logic, or lack of it, without being abusive.
- Be enthusiastic and enjoy the debate.

The language of debating

Here are some suggested words and phrases that will help you to produce strong and confident debating language.

Obviously the learned opposition . . .
If we can believe . . .
Apparently we're expected to believe that . . .
Clearly the opposition has lost all sense of direction . . .
Surely we can't be expected to believe . . .
It is easy to see the irrelevance . . .
The opposition is undoubtedly introducing irrelevancies . . .
The conclusion is inescapable . . .
The facts are simple . . .
I know you'll agree with me . . .
Our evidence, as presented to you, shows conclusively . . .
My colleagues have clearly established . . .

Time to think

To become a successful and confident debater it is important to practise the techniques outlined above. Organise some debates within your class using some of the topics suggested below, or any others that interest you and your classmates.

General/Philosophical
- Greed may be ugly, but it creates results.
- A free spirit cannot be caged.
- Life after death? We're all dying to find out.
- Meat is murder.
- Poverty is always with us.
- Prejudice is part of the human condition.
- Everyone has a right to voice an opinion.
- Human beings are innately evil.
- Religion is becoming irrelevant.
- Nature is too great for man.
- Curves are necessary.

Issue-based
- Advertising does more harm than good.
- Adopted children should have knowledge of their natural parents.
- Natural therapies are destined to replace traditional medicine.
- Television and video violence should be banned.
- De-institutionalisation of mentally ill people should occur.
- It is the government's responsibility to provide for homeless youth.
- Adolescence is the most difficult time in life.
- Smoking anywhere should be banned.
- Human beings need to protect their future from information technology.
- Capital punishment should be re-introduced in Australia.
- School uniform should be compulsory.

★ A debate is a demanding test of your oral skills, knowledge and wit, not an assessment of your personal views.

★ Debates are assessed in the areas of Matter (content), Manner and Method.

★ Research skills, an understanding of persuasive techniques, a clear vision of your purpose, and knowledge of how best to present yourself are all requirements of a successful debating technique.

18 Issues in film

The Emerald Forest

*A few tribes have never had contact with the outside world.
They still know what we have forgotten*

The Emerald Forest

So far you have been considering your own point of view, and those of others, through a study of the written word. The visual medium of film is a very powerful and dramatic means of conveying a point of view to an audience. The images are supplied for you, so you do not have to rely on your mind to construct them. The images, constructed by someone else, have an immediate impact on your existing attitudes and views.

In film, the scenes set before you express views that result from the combined contributions of writers, actors, directors, producers, cinematographers, sound editors, photographers and script editors. Each of these people comes to the film with ideas and beliefs of his or her own about the purpose of the film. When a film deals with a subject that has global relevance, the purpose might be to provoke thought and action in the audience. If this is the case, the ideas must be put together in such a way that the audience feels compelled to start thinking about the issues raised in the film. Before this can happen, however, the script must have been written, directed and produced in a way that attracts as large an audience as possible.

The Emerald Forest

Produced and Directed by John Boorman
Written by Rospo Pallenberg
Executive Producer   Edgar F. Gross
Co-produced by Michael Dryhurst
Starring   Powers Boothe, Meg Foster, Charley Boorman
Embassy Films Associates
Running Time   Approximately 1 hour 49 minutes

The Emerald Forest is available on video. The exercises in this chapter should be completed with access to a viewing of the film. It is best to view the entire film first, then to study it closely, scene by scene, using a VCR.

At the beginning of the film we are told that, 'This film was made in the rainforest of the Amazon and is based on real events and actual characters'. Briefly, the story deals with logging in the Amazon and the survival of primitive tribes within the forest. The Indians are shown living *with* the forest, not *against* it. They live for survival, enjoyment of life, and respect for their traditions.

Time to think

1 Before viewing the film, it will be useful to explore your existing knowledge of the subject by answering the questions below.
   - How extensive or limited is your understanding of the issues surrounding logging of rainforests?
   - Can you locate the Amazon region on a map of the world?
   - Where in Australia is logging a serious issue?
   - 'Global warming' is a term that is becoming more familiar to us. What is your understanding of the term?

- Are you aware of the relationship between global warming and logging of forests around the world?
- What relevance does the issue of logging have to our daily survival?
- Conservationists and timber workers both have a case to argue in the issue of logging of forests. In point form, write down the main arguments for each side.
- The quotation at the beginning of this chapter implies that 'civilised' human beings have forgotten something. What do you think it is?

First impressions

Your first impressions of a film can be the most lasting and the most valid. They are spontaneous and immediate, and express reactions that reflect your emotional and intellectual response to a film, rather than interpretations you apply from later analysis or reflection. Initial reactions are fresh and honest.

Time to think

1 In no more than 300 words, write down your first impressions after viewing *The Emerald Forest*. Use the questions below as a guide.
- Were you moved by the film?
- Did you become emotionally involved with the story or the characters?
- What is the most memorable part of the film for you?
- Did you learn anything from the film?
- Was there a message in the film?

Responding to the film

The questions in the section below have been organised into groups that relate to such things as information, comprehension, points of view, audience and purpose, and problem solving. Your class can be divided into groups, with each group allotted one group of questions on which to focus. Each group should then report back to the class on its response to the questions.

Time to think

Read the questions below before watching the film for a second time. This will help you to know what to look for in your note taking.

1 *Information — Facts — Details*
- The music at the beginning of the film establishes a particular mood. Describe this mood, making reference to the visual images that accompany the music.

- Bill is in charge of a project for a construction company. For what purpose is the forest being destroyed by that company?
- Why is it easy for the bulldozers to push over the trees?
- The abduction of Tomme is set in the past. The majority of the action takes place in the present. How many years after Tomme's abduction is the main action set? Why is the family continuing the search?
- The photographer suggests that his editor has a particular reason for his interest in the story of Tomme. What is this reason?
- According to Oovay, the photographer, how much of the world's oxygen is produced in the Amazon?
- Which two tribes in the forest have had no contact with the outside world?
- The sound of the toucan is a signal. Explain this signal.
- Why do The Fierce Ones move to The Invisible People's part of the world?
- What is the importance of the sacred stones?
- 'They are taking the skin off the world . . .
  How will she breathe?'
  What is the meaning of these lines?
- Why do the men from The Bat People help Tomme?
- The three tribes mentioned in the film are The Invisible People, The Fierce Ones, and The Bat People. What are the characteristics that cause these tribes to have these names?
- How do Tomme and The Invisible People cause a flood?
- Explain the meaning of the following terms:
  The Edge of the World
  The Dead World
  The Termite People
- At the very end of the film some details are provided on the Amazon forest and the Indians living within it. These details have significance for the world. Explain why.

2 *Viewing and Comprehension*
- Do you think the film has been given an appropriate title? Why?
- Termites are used as a symbol three times within the film. After a careful examination of dialogue and visual imagery, suggest what the termites symbolise and explain their significance to The Invisible People.
- Describe the relationship between Tomme and Daddee, and Tomme and Father.
- Both the chief of The Fierce Ones and the chief of The Invisible People describe Bill as a man of courage. What qualities in Bill have led these men from very different tribes to the same conclusion?
- The position of the girls from The Invisible People in the construction camp is the ultimate in degradation. The girls from The Fierce Ones don't appear to be affected in the same way. What has caused this difference in reaction? To help you with your answer, recall the scenes with The Fierce Ones, Bill and Oovay.
- What are the differences between The Invisible People and The Fierce Ones? Consider the following: aggression; treatment of women; attitude towards,

and use of, weapons; importance of traditions; treatment of the dead; respect for nature.
- Examine the following quotations and write down their meanings:

    If I tell a man what to do and what not to do I am no longer chief.

    (Wanadi, Chief of The Invisible People, to Bill)

    Your time has come to die.

    (Wanadi to Tomme)

    Without our women we will be people no more.

    (Wanadi to Tomme)

    When a dream becomes flesh . . . trouble is not far behind.

    (Wanadi to Tomme)

- Both Tomme and Daddee meet their spirit animals. In what way is the spirit animal important to The Invisible People? Provide an example.
- The impact of white civilisation on the tribes of the Amazon is evident in the film. Write a detailed description of the impact of white civilisation on each of the three tribes in the film.

3 *Audience and Purpose*
- In the early scenes a series of visual contrasts has been established. What are these contrasts and what is their purpose in the film?
- When Bill first realises that Tomme is missing, he makes a frantic attempt to push his way through the forest. In contrast to this, the forest appeared inviting to Tomme. In fact, he says he is not afraid of the forest. What emotional impact does this contrast have on you?
- It is usual for a director to use the forces of emotion to have an impact on the audience. The innocence of children is often a device used by writers and directors to sustain audience interest. *The Emerald Forest* is no exception. How has the innocence of children been used as a device to appeal to the audience?
- The role of the photographer, Oovay, is short lived. Why has the writer included this character in the script?
- What is the role of The Fierce Ones in the film? In particular consider the bordello and construction camp scenes. Describe your reaction to this tribe.
- While at the Dead World, Father shoots an arrow at a grader. Why has this scene been included?
- Think about why *The Emerald Forest* was written. Read the introduction of this chapter then write half a page explaining your reactions to the film and stating whether or not you now feel compelled to take action on the issue of the destruction of rainforests.

4 *Conflicts — Issues — Points of view*
- Tomme was born into a white family, but the majority of his life has been spent with a primitive tribe. When Tomme reaches manhood he asks for Kachiri as his wife. As a sign of possession he clubs Kachiri. In the so-called

civilised white society into which he was born this is not accepted practice. Tomme has been able to overcome the forces of his blood connections to conform to the traditions of this primitive society. To work out this inner conflict, Tomme might consult his spirit guide. Write a dialogue between Tomme and his spirit guide, showing how he resolves the conflict.

- Below are some of the issues raised in *The Emerald Forest*.
    Innocence versus corruption
    The destruction of the Amazon
    Survival of primitive tribes
    The abandonment of children
    Traditional livelihood versus hard-nosed commercialism

    Imagine that you are either the writer, the director, an actor or a camera operator. Write a letter to the producer of the film expessing your point of view on one of the issues above. Highlight what you have learnt about the Amazon through your involvement with the film.

- A focus throughout the film is the character of Bill. How does the film show a gradual change in his attitude towards the environment? Consider dialogue, close-ups, camera angles, and Bill's actions. What causes Bill to see his work from another point of view? Imagine yourself as the editor of Oovay's magazine. Write an informative piece on Bill.

- Below are some of the comments Tomme and Daddee make to one another. It appears that Daddee experiences some difficulty adjusting to the realisation that Tomme clearly sees himself as a natural member of The Invisible People's tribe. Write a dialogue between Tomme and Daddee in which each one reveals his position and point of view.

    T   *You live in there, when I dream.*
          Now you are here.

    T   *This is my home. It will be the home of my children.*

    T   *Why are you so sad?*
    D   *Ten years Tomme . . . looking for you . . . all over.*

    T   *Yes, it is good to hunt . . . to track an animal . . . you should be happy . . . but no, you feel sad.*
          It will be a good feast tonight.

    T   *If that is a log jam . . .*
          Water can break it.
    D   *No.*
    T   *A great flood of water can break it.*
    D   *No?*
          Not this kind of log jam.
    T   *You remember*
          The frogs sing and it rains.
          We will ask the frogs to sing very loud.

5 *Solving problems for the future*

The film presents you with a number of problems for the future. One is described below. Read and discuss this problem in groups, then work out and write down possible solutions to this problem. Use the questions that follow as a guide.

Water is necessary for the survival of any population. The most effective means of storing water is the construction of dams. The construction of dams in the Amazon rainforest is not only destroying the forest, but it is having devastating effects on the tribes within it. For some of these tribes, contact with the outside world is unknown. Four million Indians once lived there: 120 000 remain. These small tribes do not have the means of destroying the forest; they have always lived with the forest. They cannot compete with machinery.

The world needs oxygen. The Amazon rainforest provides 40 per cent of the world's oxygen, yet the forests are disappearing at the rate of 5000 acres per day. The issue is a multi-layered one of survival.

- What is the present situation?
- Who and what is being affected by that situation?
- What are the effects?
- Who has the power to bring about a change to the current course of events?
- If this situation is now a problem, what was the original set of circumstances that caused its implementation?
- What are the parts of the problem that are easy to solve?
- Which parts of the problem present difficulties?
- If the current situation is altered in any way, who will be affected?
- A range of attitudes exists towards the situation. List the attitudes, and for each one suggest a solution.
- Brainstorm the range of solutions to the problem (see Chapter 12).
- Decide on a group or individual to whom you should present your findings.
- Present your findings, as a report, to the group you have selected. This should be a persuasive piece of writing designed to influence the group to protect and preserve the planet for the future.

★ **Films are a powerful means of conveying a message to a very large audience.**

★ **A film is written and produced with a clear purpose and audience in mind and provides readily accessible ideas and information that invite an audience to respond.**

19

Problem solving

Creative critical thinking

I am a thinker — and I enjoy thinking.

Edward de Bono

Problems confront you every day of your lives. You will not always be ready for them, nor will you always know how to deal with them.

What is a problem?

A problem is often the result of a conflict of needs, concerns, backgrounds or fears between two people. What is a problem for one, may be a solution for another. People see things in different ways. For example, a fourteen-year-old boy who wishes to meet his friends at a McDonald's restaurant and then walk to the local disco, might find himself in conflict with his parents. The boy is wanting some independence, but his parents see potential problems and insist on him being driven to the disco. The solution to the problem lies in compromise. Neither party might be entirely happy, but each has considered the needs and concerns of the other.

Many problems that occur in everyday life place you in a dilemma — a situation in which a choice has to be made between two equally undesirable alternatives. The simple domestic problem outlined below illustrates how difficult it can be to arrive at a satisfactory solution.

> **The boy next door is having a party. It is his twenty first birthday. He likes loud music and has noisy friends. Your 90-year-old great grandmother has just come to stay, and needs to rest after having had an operation on her ears. Her ears are very sensitive. By 9.30 p.m. she is distraught. She cannot sleep and the noise is becoming louder. Your next-door neighbours are enjoying themselves immensely. You can tell by the noise. If you are on good terms with your neighbours, there will be no problem. You can go and talk to them, the music will be turned down, and your great grandmother can sleep. If, however, you are enemies, you will report the noise to the police. The party is creating noise pollution and disturbance of the peace. The police will arrive. The music will be turned down. Your relationship with your neighbours will worsen. What happens if you like the music and like your great grandmother as well?**

Problem solving

In amicable solving of problems, several factors are important, including goodwill on both sides and a knowledge of relevant laws. This is relatively easy with minor problems such as the one outlined above. The difficulty comes when problems arise between large groups of people, or between people of different races or countries with historical enmities. Then major problems can occur. There have been times in history when disputes have been settled only when one side admits defeat. It is better if the resolution is by compromise, where both sides think they have gained enough. This is called a win/win situation.

In much of your study you will be concerned with problem solving — the interpretation of passages in literature, solutions for mathematical problems, analysis of historical documents, or investigation of scientific material. The information discussed below can be applied in a variety of areas.

THE THINKING APPROACH

Edward de Bono proposes a way of thinking that deals with problems and provides logical steps to work through them. If we could use the following approach for all the problems that confront us, the impact of those problems might be lessened.

Problems are usually not deliberately created. As de Bono puts it,

> A problem is something that gets in our way. Problems present themselves. A task is something that you set up for yourself because you want to get somewhere.
>
> In both problems and tasks there is a starting position and a place where we want to get — but we do not know how to get there.

Solving problems is easier if you follow a process or strategy and focus on the desired result. The thinking approach to problem solving involves the steps listed below.

- Identify the problem.
- Define key terminology in the problem, if necessary.
- Break down the problem into its separate parts.
- Identify the causes of the problem.
- Identify the effects of the problem.
- Explore a range of solutions.
- Test the solutions and find the parts of each solution that would not work.
- Select the most appropriate solution to the problem.
- State why this solution is the most appropriate.

Time to think

1 Listed below are some everyday problems. With a partner, practise using the thinking approach outlined above to devise some solutions.
- Dogs are a nuisance in your school grounds. They cause confusion in sports matches, eat students' lunches, and spread rubbish from bins. What could you do to solve the problem?

- Unreturned library books are a great financial loss to libraries, and an inconvenience to other borrowers. Analyse the reasons for the existence of this problem. How do you think it can be solved?
- In a supermarket you have seen a poorly dressed woman with two small children popping sweets into the pockets of her coat. What are you going to do about it? Give reasons for your actions.
- The food in your school canteen is really unsuitable for healthy-diet-conscious students, but it sells well, and brings in money for the school. What steps can you take to improve the situation?
- You know that one of your friends has taken a valuable textbook from another student whom you do not like. The book is necessary for school studies, but is out of print. What will you do to correct this situation? Give the reasons for your actions.
- You love native birds. Your sister's cat, which she really loves, is always catching and killing them. Your sister refuses to have her cat confined at night. Outline steps you can take to satisfy both of you.
- Kangaroos are protected animals. Farmer Jones faces drought and has had to reduce his stock numbers considerably. However, the number of kangaroos feeding on his farm is increasing rapidly. What can be done to save him from financial ruin?

2 Here is a task requiring extensive, exploratory and thoughtful discussion. Read the list of issues below and use the questions that follow as a guide for your discussion. The class will need to be divided into a number of smaller groups.
Homelessness
Aboriginal land rights
Release of a convicted criminal from gaol
Imprisonment of politicians and public figures for defrauding the State or Commonwealth

Literacy among children
  Teenage suicide
- List the problems associated with the situation selected by your group.
- What are the causes of the situation?
- What are the consequences of the situation?
- Who will be affected by the situation or by decisions made within it?
- There is a range of ways in which the people concerned might be affected. Discuss the people, their relationship to or involvement in the scenario, and how they will be affected. It might be useful to draw up a chart using the following headings:
  Person
  Occupation or relationship
  How affected in short term
  How affected in long term
- It might be useful to take a historical perspective and consider the origins of the situation, or how similar problems were handled in the past.
- Consider that the solution might involve prevention.
- Report your findings to the class.

★ **Problems are an inevitable part of human existence and can result from conflicts about needs, concerns, backgrounds, or fears between people.**

★ **Problem solving requires clear and creative thinking and is usually easier if you follow a process or strategy and concentrate on the desired result.**

Part Three

On assignment

This section looks at some of the issues affecting societies today. It provides material to allow you to take on the role of an investigative journalist and to work out your own view on each subject.

20
Human rights

There is no greater injustice in the world than an innocent child being denied that most basic of human rights, the right to sufficient food to sustain life.

Pamela Bone *Age,* 18 April 1994

The material in this chapter has been selected to show that events in world history recur. The time and place might be different, but the effect is the same.

The Australian Concise Oxford Dictionary defines human rights as 'rights held to be justifiably claimed by any person'. The *World Human Rights Guide*, compiled by Charles Humana, defines human rights as 'the laws, customs, and practices that have evolved over the centuries to protect ordinary people, minorities, groups, and races from oppressive rulers and governments.'

Time to think

1 Read the United Nations' *Universal Declaration of Human Rights* and answer the questions that follow.

Universal Declaration of Human Rights

Adopted by the UN General Assembly in 1948 without a dissenting vote

Article 1
All human beings are born free and equal in dignity and rights. They are endowed with reason and conscience and should act towards one another in a spirit of brotherhood.

Article 2
Everyone is entitled to all the rights and freedoms set forth in this Declaration, without distinction of any kind, such as race, colour, sex, language, religion, political or other opinion, national or social origin, property, birth or other status.

Furthermore, no distinction shall be made on the basis of the political, jurisdictional or international status of the country or territory to which a person belongs, whether it be independent, trust, non-self-governing or under any other limitation of sovereignty.

Article 3
Everyone has the right to life, liberty and the security of person.

Article 4
No one shall be held in slavery or servitude; slavery and the slave trade shall be prohibited in all their forms.

Article 5
No one shall be subjected to torture or to cruel, inhuman or degrading treatment or punishment.

Article 6
Everyone has the right to recognition everywhere as a person before the law.

Article 7
All are equal before the law and are entitled without any discrimination to equal protection of the law. All are entitled to equal protection against any discrimination in violation of this Declaration and against any incitement to such discrimination.

Article 8
Everyone has the right to an effective remedy by the competent national tribunals for acts violating the fundamental rights granted him by the constitution or by law.

Article 9
No one shall be subjected to arbitrary arrest, detention or exile.

Article 10
Everyone is entitled in full equality to a fair and public hearing by an independent and impartial tribunal, in the determination of his rights and obligations and of any criminal charge against him.

Article 11
1 Everyone charged with a penal offence has the right to be presumed innocent until proved guilty according to law in a public trial at which he has had all the guarantees necessary for his defence.
2 No one shall be held guilty of any penal offence on account of any act or omission which did not constitute a penal offence, under national or international law, at the time when it was committed. Nor shall a heavier penalty be imposed than the one that was applicable at the time the penal offence was committed.

Article 12
No one shall be subjected to arbitrary interference with his privacy, family, home or correspondence, nor to attacks upon his honour and reputation. Everyone has the right to the protection of the law against such interference or attacks.

Article 13
1 Everyone has the right to freedom of movement and residence within the borders of each state.
2 Everyone has the right to leave any country, including his own, and to return to his country.

Article 14
1 Everyone has the right to seek and to enjoy in other countries asylum from persecution.
2 This right may not be invoked in the case of prosecutions genuinely arising from non-political crimes or from acts contrary to the purposes and principles of the United Nations.

Article 15
1 Everyone has the right to a nationality.
2 No one shall be arbitrarily deprived of his nationality nor denied the right to change his nationality.

Article 16
1 Men and women of full age, without any limitation due to race, nationality or religion, have the right to marry and to found a family. They are entitled to equal rights as to marriage, during marriage and at its dissolution.
2 Marriage shall be entered into only with the free and full consent of the intending spouses.
3 The family is the natural and fundamental group unit of society and is entitled to protection by society and the State.

Article 17
1 Everyone has the right to own property alone as well as in association with others.
2 No one shall be arbitrarily deprived of his property.

Article 18
Everyone has the right to freedom of thought, conscience and religion; this right includes freedom to change his religion or belief, and freedom, either alone or in community with others and in public or private, to manifest his religion or belief in teaching, practice, worship and observance.

Article 19
Everyone has the right to freedom of opinion and expression; this right includes freedom to hold opinions without interference and to seek, receive and impart information and ideas through any media and regardless of frontiers.

Article 20
1 Everyone has the right to freedom of peaceful assembly and association.
2 No one may be compelled to belong to an association.

Article 21
1 Everyone has the right to take part in the government of his country, directly or through freely chosen representatives.
2 Everyone has the right of equal access to public service in his country.
3 The will of the people shall be the basis of the authority of government; this will shall be expressed in periodic and genuine elections which shall be by universal and equal suffrage and shall be held by secret vote or by equivalent free voting procedures.

Article 22
Everyone, as a member of society, has the right to social security and is entitled to realization, through national effort and international co-operation and in accordance with the organization and resources of each State, of the economic, social and cultural rights indispensable for his dignity and the free development of his personality.

Article 23
1 Everyone has the right to work, to free choice of employment, to just and favourable conditions of work and to protection against unemployment.
2 Everyone, without any discrimination, has the right to equal pay for equal work.
3 Everyone who works has the right to just and favourable renumeration [sic] ensuring for himself and his family an existence worthy of human dignity, and supplemented, if necessary, by other means of social protection.
4 Everyone has the right to form and to join trade unions for the protection of his interests.

Article 24
Everyone has the right to rest and leisure, including reasonable limitation of working hours and periodic holidays with pay.

Article 25
1 Everyone has the right to a standard of living adequate for the health and well-being of himself and of his family, including food, clothing, housing and medical care and necessary social services, and the right to security in the event of unemployment, sickness, disability, widowhood, old age or other lack of livelihood in circumstances beyond his control.
2 Motherhood and childhood are entitled to special care and assistance. All children, whether born in or out of wedlock, shall enjoy the same social protection.

Article 26
1 Everyone has the right to education. Education shall be free, at least in the elementary and fundamental stages. Elementary education shall be compulsory. Technical and professional education shall be made generally available and higher education shall be equally accessible to all on the basis of merit.
2 Education shall be directed to the full development of the human personality and to the strengthening of respect for human rights and fundamental freedoms. It shall promote understanding, tolerance and friendship among all nations, racial or religious groups, and shall further the activities of the United Nations for the maintenance of peace.
3 Parents have a prior right to choose the kind of education that shall be given to their children.

Article 27
1 Everyone has the right freely to participate in the cultural life of the community, to enjoy the arts and to share in scientific advancement and its benefits.
2 Everyone has the right to the protection of the moral and material interests resulting from any scientific, literary, or artistic production of which he is the author.

> **Article 28**
> Everyone is entitled to a social and international order in which the rights and freedoms set forth in this Declaration can be fully realized.
>
> **Article 29**
> 1 Everyone has duties to the community in which alone the free and full development of his personality is possible.
> 2 In the exercise of his rights and freedoms, everyone shall be subject only to such limitations as are determined by law solely for the purpose of securing due recognition and respect for the rights and freedoms of others and of meeting the just requirements of morality, public order and the general welfare in a democratic society.
> 3 These rights and freedoms may in no case be exercised contrary to the purposes and principles of the United Nations.
>
> **Article 30**
> Nothing in this Declaration may be interpreted as implying for any State, group or person any right to engage in any activity or to perform any act aimed at the destruction of any of the rights and freedoms set forth herein.

- The *Universal Declaration of Human Rights* was adopted by the United Nations in 1948. In the context of world history, what do you think prompted this action?
- Using your dictionaries find definitions for each of the following words (the number in brackets indicates the Article in which the word appears):

endowed (1)	exile (9)
conscience (1)	impartial (10)
brotherhood (1)	omission (11,2)
jurisdictional (2)	asylum (14,1)
independent (2)	invoked (14,2)
sovereignty (2)	manifest (18)
prohibited (4)	compelled (20,2)
degrading (5)	suffrage (21,3)
incitement (7)	indispensable (22)
tribunals (8)	remuneration (23,3)
fundamental (8)	tolerance (26,2)
arbitrary (9)	democratic (29,2)

- What is your view on the overall purpose of the Declaration?
- Carefully read Article 10. Discuss its meaning with a partner. Together think of incidents at an international level, a national level, and a local level, which suggest that Article 10 has been upheld. Note the incidents in your books.
- Carefully read Article 19, then rewrite it in your own words. Think of incidents at an international level, a national level, and a local level, which suggest that Article 19 has been violated. Note the incidents in your books.
- Have a close look at the way the Declaration has been expressed. It makes use of words such as *everyone*, *no one* and *all*. Write your own Declaration of Rights for Students in Secondary Schools. Consider areas such as bullying, choosing subjects, making mistakes, equality of opportunity. There are many

more. Think about the order in which you place them and label them Article 1, Article 2, and so on.

2 Read Pamela Bone's article, 'Words and Excuses Fail When Children Are Innocent Victims' (*Age*, 25 July 1994), and answer the questions that follow.

Words and excuses fail when children are innocent victims

MY FRIEND, who works for World Vision, was tired and angry. 'There are babies there with no parents, there is nothing to feed them on, and one by one they will die. They can put a man on the moon but they can't get in there and save those children,' she yelled over the telephone.

My friend, whose name is Glenda Orland, thought I should write a column about Rwanda. 'I don't know what I could say,' I said.

Recently I saw on a news program that a group of Rwandan refugees had taken over a psychiatric hospital. Because the refugees were frightened of the patients they had locked them into a room and left them there for days without food or water.

The television camera showed the hands of the patients reaching through the bars, imploring. A British doctor from Oxfam or some other agency told the reporter: 'I don't know what to say about people who could do this to other human beings. I really don't.' Then he turned his head away to hide the tears. I don't know what to say about such people either.

Strange how we always expect victims to be good people. Who are the victims in Rwanda? Hutu women have admitted beating to death their neighbor's children because they were Tutsi. What can anyone say about that? Most of the million or so Rwandan refugees who have fled into neighboring Zaire, where they are now dying in their thousands of hunger, dehydration and disease, are Hutus. They fled because they fear retribution from the Tutsi-led army for the genocide of half a million Tutsi civilians during the past three months of civil war. There is little doubt that among the refugees there are people who helped to commit that genocide.

The quote on my desk calendar as I begin to write this says 'Fear is the parent of cruelty – J.A. Froude'. So it is fear that drives people to commit such atrocities. That was the excuse the Nazis used; that if they didn't help kill the Jews they would be punished. We didn't excuse them.

What kind of people can kill children simply because of their ethnicity? Glenda says that if the allies had lost World War II, if the Japanese had taken over Australia, and if the Japanese had all the privileges and were treating us like serf as the Hutus claim the Tutsi did to them, we might be killing each other now.

There have been several programs on television recently about the Jewish holocaust. Again, pictures of children, this time not starving, naked black children, but children neatly dressed in coats and shoes and socks being marched off to gas ovens. Unspeakable; monstrous. (Worse,

(continued)

because of its cold-bloodedness, than the beating to death of Rwandan children by their neighbors? No, nothing's worse or better when you talk about the murder of children). And the people who murdered the Jewish children were members of a society that thought itself the most civilised in the world.

The fact that genocide happened in Germany 50 years ago, is happening in Bosnia and Rwanda today, shows that any race could do it, given a particular set of circumstances. Could any individual do it? I doubt it. I refuse to believe I could ever beat a child to death. No doubt you believe the same about yourself, and we are both probably right. What has happened in Rwanda is an aberration of human nature, not its norm. But could we may [sic] make that claim with as much confidence if we lived in a country that was not free and democratic, with a high value on human rights, and if we had been fed hatred along with our mothers' milk?

There are no innocent victims in war, some philosopher (I think Jean Paul Sartre) said. What nonsense. The majority of the Rwandan refugees are victims of war, not war criminals. As one Hutu refugee said, 'six million Rwandans are not killers'. What is certain is that the children – up to 100 000 of them orphaned or separated from their parents – are innocent.

The international community is coming to the aid of Rwanda, as it always does when it knows it has to, when the tragedy becomes impossible for the media to ignore. Glenda, who arranges publicity for World Vision, gets cynical sometimes about the fickleness of the media. 'They'll be crawling all over it (Rwanda) like ants for a couple of weeks', she said. Meanwhile, in Sudan, Angola and Mozambique millions of people are quietly starving.

If the media had not been there in Germany 50 years ago, taking pictures when the death camps were opened, there would be a lot more people now than the few cranks there are, denying the holocaust happened. That is why the media are needed in Rwanda today. (I don't have to tell Glenda that, of course).

The response of the international community is too late for many thousands of Rwandans. Why, as Glenda said, 25 years after men walked on the moon, is it beyond the world's capacity to stop such tragedies from happening with such appalling frequency? Why couldn't the amount of time, money and energy that went into the space program be put into making the earth a safer and fairer place?

Unlike Glenda, I'm old enough to remember that 25 years ago people were asking the same questions. The trouble is that while the moon landing had a specific, ideological goal (to better the Russians), the task of preventing wars and ending hunger is far more nebulous. It doesn't have the same elements of excitement, competition and boys' own adventure. But if it was worth anything, the moon landing, the ability to see the whole Earth from outer space, should have convinced people of the oneness of humanity. A pity it hasn't.

There, Glenda, I did think of something to say. Whether anything you or I could say would ever make a damned bit of difference is another matter.

- What are the main points made by the writer?
- A writer writes with a purpose in mind (see Chapter 4). In your opinion, what is Pamela Bone's purpose?
- Would you describe the writer's approach to her subject as personal or impersonal? Support your view with evidence from the article.
- Much of the information is presented in an anecdotal manner. Do you find this effective? Explain your response.

- Identify an analogy made by the writer (see Chapter 11). Why has this been included?
- Time is mentioned in the article — '50 years ago' and '25 years ago'. Why does the writer do this?
- Explain the meaning of the words, 'There are no innocent victims in war . . .'. Describe the writer's reaction to this.
- In what way is Glenda cynical about the media?
- Describe the tone adopted by the writer. Is it based on compassion, anger, resignation, futility, or something else?
- Reread the *Universal Declaration of Human Rights*. What evidence can you find in 'Words and Excuses Fail When Children Are Innocent Victims' of the violation of human rights in Rwanda?

3 Read the two extracts and the article below and answer the questions that follow. The extracts below come from the novel, *Night* (a record of childhood in the death camps of Auschwitz and Buchenwald), by Elie Wiesel (1944).

'Poor devils, you're going to the crematory.'

He seemed to be telling the truth. Not far from us, flames were leaping up from a ditch, gigantic flames. They were burning something. A lorry drew up at the pit and delivered its load — little children. Babies! Yes, I saw it — saw it with my own eyes . . . those children in the flames. (Is it surprising that I could not sleep after that? Sleep had fled from my eyes.) So this was where we were going. A little farther on was another and larger ditch for adults.

I pinched my face. Was I still alive? Was I awake? I could not believe it. How could it be possible for them to burn people, children, and for the world to keep silent? No, none of this could be true. It was a nightmare . . . Soon I should wake with a start, my heart pounding, and find myself back in the bedroom of my childhood, among my books . . .

(page 43)

His voice was terribly sad. I realized that he did not want to see what they were going to do to me. He did not want to see the burning of his only son.

My forehead was bathed in cold sweat. But I told him that I did not believe that they could burn people in our age, that humanity would never tolerate it . . .

'Humanity? Humanity is not concerned with us. Today anything is allowed. Anything is possible, even these crematories . . .'

(page 44)

> Never shall I forget that night, the first night in camp, which has turned my life into one long night... Never shall I forget that smoke. Never shall I forget the little faces of the children, whose bodies I saw turned into wreaths of smoke beneath a silent blue sky.
>
> Never shall I forget those flames which consumed my faith forever.
>
> Never shall I forget that nocturnal silence which deprived me, for all eternity, of the desire to live. Never shall I forget those moments which murdered my God and my soul and turned my dreams to dust. Never shall I forget these things, even if I am condemned to live as long as God Himself. Never.
>
> **(page 45)**

The extracts below come from 'Life, Death and the News' (*New Woman*, June 1993), an article by Jeffrey Goodell based on an interview with Gordana Knezevic, a journalist living in Sarajevo in 1993.

> 'Life in Sarajevo is prehistoric,' she says. 'People spend all day hunting for food and trying to stay alive. We are chopping down trees for firewood, burying our dead in our front yards because it is too dangerous to visit the cemetery.' She ticks off a litany of horrors: the shelling of hospitals and schools, the hundreds of wounded children who've lost arms and legs, the thousands of Muslims and Croats starving in concentration camps. So far, since the war has broken out, more than 200 000 people have been declared dead or missing, and 2.5 million have been forced out of their homes. 'This is not a civil war in my country,' she says. 'This is genocide at its worst.'
>
> **(page 102)**

> But, as Knezevic well knows, dodging bullets in the name of journalism is one thing; it is quite another when you are a mother of three children. When the war began, she and her husband, a philosophy professor at Sarajevo University, made arrangements for their children to take refuge. Olga, 7, and Igor, 15, agreed to stay with friends in London. But Boris, 13, wouldn't leave Sarajevo. Like all kids in the city, Boris now leads a closeted life; since the fighting started, he has not left the apartment building. He spends most of the day surrounded by buckets, waiting to catch the water that, with luck, may flow from the faucets. When the shelling comes, Boris grabs his diary and his Guns 'N Roses tapes and dives straight for the basement.
>
> **(page 105)**

The article below is from the *Age*, 25 July 1994.

Baby Amina joins Rwanda's Darwinian tussle

A mother, dying from cholera, and her child at the Munigi camp outside Goma. Orphanages in the area are hopelessly overcrowded.

By DELE OLOJEDE
Goma, Zaire, Sunday

Nobody knew her name or where she came from, so a new identity had been assigned to her by Mr Kevin Noone, a relief worker for the Irish group GOAL. 'This is the fifth orphanage I have tried since last night', said Mr Noone, cradling 15-month-old Amina, found crying next to a pile of bodies which included her parents.

The temporary shelters arranged for children lost in the Rwandan refugee maelstrom have been overwhelmed in recent days. Thousands have been separated from their families; hundreds have lost their parents to the epidemic, and they roam the dusty streets of Goma searching for food.

Mr Noone said he found Amina on Friday night, suffering from diarrhoea. He took her, with four other children, in search of emergency facilities. The other children, older and healthier, found a place relatively easily. But Amina was too young and sick and orphanages had no one who could care for her at that time of night.

Mr Noone kept her Friday night and started making the rounds again on Saturday. At Caritas orphanage, run by Sisters of St Joseph, a Spanish order, dozens of similarly fated children received care in frightful conditions, many lying in their vomit. Mr Noone was advised that Amina be taken to another place where she stood a better chance of survival.

Which left only the SOS village, 14.5 kilometres west of Goma, where 2500 children had already been left since more than one million Rwandan refugees arrived last week. The centre had been

(continued)

built for only 40 children, but French troops helped clear the surrounding cassava farm and aid agencies brought in tents.

As Amina waited to be evaluated, three trucks came rumbling in filled with another 200 children. 'They are coming so fast, we can't cope,' said Mr Osei Kofi, a UNICEF official. 'We started with 50 on Monday, now we have more than 4000.'

There is a shortage of everything. 'If we don't have water; all the kids are going to die,' said Dr Ninet Lalani.

Mr Noone stepped into a room in which 24 children Amina's age had been placed – and flinched. The babies, all painfully tiny, some crying but most too weak even for that, did not appear to stand much of a chance for survival.

'I am not leaving her here,' he announced shortly, although exactly what would happen to Amina was unclear, since Mr Noone is due to leave for Croatia in eight days.

- Before rereading all of the material above, write down your first impressions, including any emotional responses you had to it.
- Look carefully at the source of each piece. Does the material provide first-hand descriptions? Can you accept the descriptions as believable?
- Each article focuses on a particular group. What is that group in each case?
- Read the articles again. List similarities in the content.
- Contained within the material above is an overall message to the world. What is this message?
- Who should hear and react to this message? Explain your reason.
- Consider the individuals described in the material. In your own words explain how each individual's life has been affected.
- There is a link between Pamela Bone's article (see pages 140–1) and the above material. What is this link?
- Look carefully at the time and place described in each of these situations. Refer again to the *Universal Declaration of Human Rights*. What comments can you make about the effect of the Declaration and the progress made by the societies in which the descriptions are set?

4 Using the information provided above and your own research, write an informative or persuasive response of approximately 600 words to one of the following topics.

Humanity is everybody's right.

Children are the innocent victims of adult actions.

21

Aborigines and Australia

He crouches and buries his face in his hands
And hides in the dark of his hair
For he cannot look up to the storm smitten clouds
Nor think of the loneliness there
Of the loss and the loneliness there

Henry Kendall, *The Last of His Tribe*

Aborigines and Australia 147

How much do you know about Aboriginal history, society and culture? Did you know, for example, that the word Aborigine means belonging to a race of tribal people? Did you also know that Aborigines have different regional names? Some of these names are: Kooris, for those living in south-eastern Australia; Murris, for those living in Queensland; Nungas, for those living in South Australia; and Nyungars, for those living in Western Australia.

Reconciliation

This section focuses on reconciliation between black and white Australians. Reconciliation involves developing an understanding of the past, and of cultural differences, and making plans for improved relationships in the future.

Below is a range of material, both historical and recent, which will provide you with a starting point for thinking about reconciliation. Follow these steps in your investigation:

- Write down everything that you know about Australian Aborigines.
- Read the information that follows carefully and thoughtfully.
- Make notes of the main points involved in the issue of reconciliation.
- Note the problems and difficulties connected with the issue.

Time to think

1 Read the material below and complete the task that follows.

The extracts below come from Manning Clark's *Select Documents in Australian History 1788–1850*.

37 Clashes Between Whites and Aborigines. 1788

A party of them, consisting of sixteen or eighteen persons, some time after landed on the island, where the people of the Sirius were preparing a garden, and with much artifice, watching their opportunity, carried off a shovel, a spade, and a pick-axe. On their being fired at and hit on the legs by one of the people with small shot, the pick-axe was dropped, but they carried off the other tools.

To such circumstances as these must be attributed the termination of that good understanding which had hitherto subsisted between us and them, and which Governor Phillip laboured to improve whenever he had an opportunity. But it might have been foreseen that this would unavoidably happen: the convicts were everywhere straggling about, collecting animals and gum to sell to the people of the transports, who at the same time were procuring spears, shields, fishing-lines and other articles from the natives to carry to Europe, the loss of which must have been attended with many inconveniences to the owners, as it was soon evident that they were the only means whereby they obtained or could procure their daily subsistence.

D. Collins

38 Tench's Sympathy with the Aborigines. 1788

Our intercourse with them was neither frequent or cordial. They seemed studiously to avoid us, either from fear, jealousy or hatred. When they met with unarmed stragglers, they sometimes killed, and sometimes wounded them . . . a farther acquaintance with them . . . led me to conclude, that the unprovoked outrages committed upon them, by unprincipled individuals among us, caused the evils we had experienced. To prevent them from being plundered of their fishing-tackle and weapons of war, a proclamation was issued, forbidding their sale among us . . .

An extraordinary calamity was now observed among the natives . . . On inspection it appeared that all the parties had died a natural death: pustules, similar to those occasioned by the small pox, were thickly spread on the bodies; but how a disease, to which our former observations had led us to suppose them strangers, could at once have introduced itself, and have spread so widely, seemed inexplicable.

W. Tench

In reply to a suggestion from Thomas Walker, on the 1888 Centennial celebrations, that, 'We ought to do something for the Aborigines,' Henry Parkes replied, 'And remind them that we have robbed them.'

The article below, 'Invasion Versus Settlement Debate Wears On' was written by Henry Reynolds (*Weekend Australian*, 13–14 August 1994).

Invasion versus settlement debate wears on

CONFLICTING historic interpretation presents reconciliation with one of its greatest problems – how to bring together the traditional narrative taught to generations of white Australians with the very different story long known to, and carefully nurtured by, Aboriginal communities.

White Australian resistance to change has focused on the critical question of whether the country was settled or invaded. This has become the chosen battleground between the old story and the new.

(*continued*)

'Most Australians', the editor of *The Weekend Australian* argued in February, 'do not accept and will never accept the denial of the legitimacy of their civilisation which the term invasion implies. It is wrong to rewrite our history so that it reflects an Aboriginal interpretation to the exclusion of an European interpretation.'

Contemporary Aborigines speak of invasion. Was this the view of their ancestors? What evidence we have suggests it was. David Collins, the principal legal officer of the new colony, realised very quickly that the Aboriginal clans around Sydney would never be reconciled to the loss of territory. He wrote: 'While they entertained the idea of our having dispossessed them of their residences, they must always consider us as enemies; and upon this principle they made a point of attacking the white people whenever opportunity and safety concurred.'

The story was the same in Tasmania. An army officer who spent several years with the Aborigines on the Bass Strait Islands in the early years of their exile concluded that they considered themselves as having been 'engaged in a justifiable war against the invaders of their country'. G. A. Robinson, who spent years in close contact with the Tasmanians, observed that: 'They consider every injury they can inflict upon the white men as an act of duty and patriotism and however much they may dread the punishment which our laws inflict on them, they consider the sufferers under those punishments as martyrs in the cause of their country.'

It would be possible to find many similar comments from observers in other parts of Australia.

The problem for those who want to quarantine these ideas as being purely 'Aboriginal' is that many colonists agreed with them. The correspondent writing to the Hobart Town Gazette in 1824 told his readers that: 'We ought to feel that we have invaded a domain from which our invasion has expelled those who were born, bred and providentially supplied in it'. The Aborigines, another colonist wrote, were 'a race of people whose crime is that of repelling the invaders of their country.' This was the way it looked from Britain. Colonel C. J. Napier, one of the most decorated soldiers of the age, closely studied the situation in the colonies in the 1830s. He had no doubt the British had invaded Australia. In a few words he wrote: 'Our conduct is simply this. By force we take away the country of the savage. When the savage resists, we put him to death by laws which he does not, and cannot, understand; those laws being contrary to his habits, written in an unknown language and within the influence of which laws we have forced him by the unjust invasion of his country.'

Why is it so difficult to accept today an interpretation of events which fair-minded colonists were comfortable with 150 years ago?

Opponents of the invasion thesis defend a number of different positions. They contrast what happened in Sydney in 1788, or Hobart in 1803-04, with other invasions and argue that the Australian case is quite different. Commentators have variously referred to the Norman invasion of 1066, the German invasion of Poland or the D-Day landing of 1944.

Another line of defence is to argue that the British never said and didn't think they were engaged in an invasion. But the test of an invasion has never been the justification or the rhetoric used by the perpetrator. Invaders rarely admit what they are about. They have variously argued that they were asserting a legitimate dynastic claim, restoring law and order, forestalling planned aggression, defending their citizens, bringing the true religion, or occupying an empty land.

THEN again, there are those who say that force was not used or the first landing contested. If there was no blood on the beaches, the argument runs, there was no invasion.

So what can we extract from the record?

The early governors were fully aware of the role that military force played in the establishment of colonies. Once the settlers had landed, any Aboriginal resistance was to be put down with as much force as required. That was fundamental to the whole venture. In Tasmania the direct application of military force was manifest. Somewhere between 400 and

(*continued*)

500 troops were in the field for five years and governor Arthur constantly demanded a second regiment to defeat the Aborigines. Governor Phillip carefully calculated how many troops he needed to meet the same challenge. Writing to the Colonial Office in 1789 that, as he now knew the nature of Aboriginal society, 'a less force will be wanted for the security of the settlement than what I considered as necessary soon after my arrival . . . I presume that a battalion of 500 men will be sufficient.'

The soldiers were used in ways totally inconsistent with peaceful settlement. The British behaved like an army of occupation. When Phillip's 'gamekeeper' McEntire was speared in December 1790 the governor sent out a punitive expedition to 'strike a decisive blow . . . and to enthuse a universal terror'. The original instructions to the military detachment were to capture two members of the clans around Botany Bay and to kill and decapitate 10 others.

Official instructions given to the Tasmanian and NSW Governors in 1825 made the situation even clearer. Lord Bathurst told the two men that when dealing with Aboriginal resistance they were 'to oppose force by force and to repel such aggressions in the same manner as if they proceeded from subjects of an accredited state.'

Martial law was imposed on the Tasmanian Aborigines and kept in place for four years. The solicitor general of the colony explained that the effect of the relevant proclamation was 'to place the Aborigines on the footing of open enemies to the king, in a state of actual warfare against him'.

The legal situation thus defined fitted comfortably with common perceptions and with popular rhetoric. Practically everyone in Tasmania, from the governor and senior military officers down, thought they were fighting a war and said so in official dispatches, private letters and speeches.

The editor of Brisbane's Moreton Bay Courier declared in 1848: 'We hold this country by the right of conquest . . . and that right gives us a just claim to its continual possession.'

'It must be constantly borne in mind,' the editor of the Queensland Guardian wrote in 1861, 'that with the white man in this country, it is a question of forced occupation or none at all'. In that same month a prominent Queensland politician addressed the local parliament, arguing that the colonists 'must be considered to be, as they always have been, at open war with the Aborigines'.

Such frank assessments of the colonial situation found their way into the work of 19th century historians. In his classic study The Australian Race, Edward Curr noted that 'in the first place the meeting of the Aboriginal tribes of Australia and the white pioneer results as a rule in war, which lasts from six months to 10 years, according to the nature of the country, the amount of settlement which takes place in the neighbourhood and the proclivities of the individuals concerned.'

It is in the face of facts like these that the critics of the invasion thesis meet their greatest difficulty, mistakenly thinking that contemporary historians have invented these ideas in order to use them in present debate. Nothing could be further from the truth. What is taken to be the true version of the past was the creation of writers in the early years of the 20th century who wanted to purge the past of its less savoury aspects in order to create a history worthy of the new nation.

How we define the actions of the colonists determines the way in which we interpret black resistance. If Australia was invaded, the Aborigines can be seen as patriotic defenders of their homeland. If it was settled, they become outlaws and rebels and their actions criminal.

THIS was appreciated as far back as the 1820s. A Tasmanian colonist writing to a Launceston newspaper in 1831 had a series of questions which challenge us today as much as they did readers of the time. 'Are these unhappy creatures the subjects of our king in a state of rebellion, or are they an injured people, whom we have invaded and with whom we are at war? Are they within the reach of our laws, or are they to be judged by the law of nations? Are they to be viewed as murderers or as prisoners of war?'

This answer is equally disturbing to those who wish to cling to the idea of

(continued)

peaceful settlement. 'We are at war with them; they look upon us as enemies – as invaders – as their oppressors and persecutors, they resist our invasions.'

Reconciliation demands that we pay as much respect to the thousands of Aborigines who died resisting the British invasion of the continent as we do to those other Australians who gave their lives in the wars of the 20th century. We can't do that if we continue to cling to the comforting myth that Australia was settled rather than invaded. Reconciliation demands that we show as much generosity of spirit as the writer of 1831 who concluded his letter in the following way:

'What we call their crime is what in a white man we should call patriotism. Where is the man amongst ourselves who would not resist an invading enemy; who would not avenge the murder of his parents, the ill usage of his wife and daughters and the spoilation of all his earthly goods by a foreign enemy, if he had an opportunity. He who would not do so, would be scouted, execrated, nay executed as a coward and a traitor; while we who did would be immortalised as a patriot. Why then shall we deny the same feelings to the blacks.'

Henry Reynolds is a professor of history at James Cook University, Townsville

The information below, 'The Key Issues of Reconciliation', comes from the Council for Aboriginal Reconciliation (*Weekend Australian*, 13–14 August 1994)

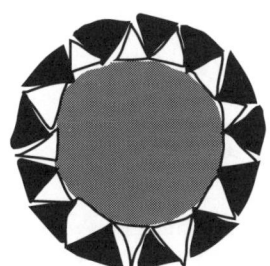

THE KEY ISSUES OF RECONCILIATION

The Council for Aboriginal Reconciliation has a clear view of the practical achievements that are necessary to bring about reconciliation between Aboriginal and Torres Strait Islander peoples and the wider community.

It has identified eight key issues which are essential to the reconciliation process. These require a practical response by the whole Australian community. Addressing these issues in a committed and effective way is essential to our future.

The key issues are:
Understanding Country: A greater understanding of the importance of land and sea in Aboriginal and Torres Strait Islander societies;
Improving Relationships: Better relationship between Aboriginal and Torres Strait Islander Australians and the wider community;
Valuing Cultures: Recognition that Aboriginal and Torres Strait Islander cultures are a valued part of Australian heritage;
Sharing Histories: A sense for all Australians of a shared ownership of their history;

Addressing Disadvantage: A greater awareness of the causes of indigenous Australians' disadvantage;

Responding to Custody Levels: A greater community response to addressing the underlying causes of the high levels of Aboriginal and Torres Strait Islander people in custody;

Agreeing on a Document: Agreement on whether the process of reconciliation would be advanced by a formal document or documents of reconciliation; and

Controlling Destinies: Greater opportunities for indigenous Australians to control their destinies.

The Council wants to know what the community thinks about these issues and how people have worked at improving their knowledge and understanding about these matters as well as any activity undertaken in a mutually co-operative manner with Aboriginal and Torres Strait Islander peoples over these issues.

It also has information and programs to encourage people to get involved. If you want information, or would like to be included on the Council's mailing list to receive a quarterly newsletter, write to:

Council for Aboriginal Reconciliation
Locked Bag 14
Queen Victoria Terrace
Parkes ACT 2600

COUNCIL FOR ABORIGINAL RECONCILIATION

The article below, 'Lily's Daughter — A Life of Hope' by Lois O'Donoghue, comes from the Council for Aboriginal Reconciliation (*Walking Together*, 1994).

Lily's Daughter: A Life of Hope

Lois O'Donoghue CBE AM, a member of the Council for Aboriginal Reconciliation, has lived a life of tenacious service. Here, the 1984 Australian of the Year tells her story.

I was born at the property 'Granite Downs' at Indulkana in South Australia. My mother was a Yunkunytjatjara woman. My father, an Irish station manager, I never knew.

When I was two I was taken away from my mother and placed in the United Aborigines' Mission at Quorn. It was called the Colbrook Home for Half-Caste Children.

My name, Lowitja, became 'Lois'. My brother and three of my sisters also were brought into the home. It was a time when white society thought this was the only way to cope with children like us.

The impact of taking a child from a mother is far more complex, more profound, than many imagine.

This was the fate of many other light-skinned Aboriginal children and in the mission some sense of family developed amongst us children.

We weren't allowed to speak our own language or to ask questions about our

(continued)

origins or our parents. But new children were constantly being brought in and, in secret, we asked about our families. I found out my mother was called 'Lily'.

The constant stream of new children coming in enabled us to maintain our Pitjantjatjara language among ourselves and to reinforce our ties with our country and our own people.

When I was 29 and working as a welfare officer and nursing sister with the South Australian Department of Aboriginal Affairs I went to Coober Pedy. In a supermarket I heard someone say 'That's Lily's daughter'.

It turned out that in the group were my mother's sister and my mother's brother and they had seen the family resemblance. They told me she was at Oodnadatta.

It took three months until I managed to get there, with my eldest sister, Eileen. Our mother had heard that I was coming and had been waiting along the road every day for weeks, from first light in the morning until dark.

For me, the meeting was a little bit of an anticlimax because it was Eileen, her first born, whom she was not expecting, that she was so overjoyed to see.

While we were in Oodnadatta our mother proudly introduced us to everyone in the town, but she carefully steered us away from the camp where she was living. She realised we'd been brought up differently and didn't want us to see her poor conditions.

Later, I was able to take my mother south to visit my brothers and sisters and her grandchildren.

These are precious memories.

I learnt many things from this contact with my mother. I learnt what hope and patience means – how she had never given up hope of seeing her children again.

I also learnt what kinship means to Aboriginal people – how in traditional society everyone has a place and a relationship with all other members of the group. These relationships help ensure that everyone is looked after. These sorts of values still prevail in Aboriginal society.

From my mother I also realised what it meant to be on the receiving end of racist policies and to have basic human rights denied – like even the right to raise one's own children.

My time at the mission, however, had opened my eyes to other things. I realised I had some ability and I wanted to do something with my life.

The positive side of being in the home was that children like us had learnt discipline and skills which enabled us to fight our way through the white system later in our lives.

Along with many other Aboriginal girls at that time, I was expected to go into domestic service. I had higher aspirations and wanted to become a nurse.

I did my initial nursing training at the South Coast District Hospital at Victor Harbour in South Australia.

It was good, but I encountered my first major obstacle when I was denied entry to the Royal Adelaide Hospital to further my training. The reason I was denied entry was that I was Aboriginal.

This was my take-off point. I was not prepared to accept this set-back.

I joined the Aboriginal Advancement League (the only organisation involved in Aboriginal rights at that time). I lobbied members of Parliament. I confronted the Premier and the matron of the hospital. I spoke in Adelaide Town Hall. Remember, this was the year 1953 – still 14 years before the 1967 referendum and any proper recognition of Aboriginal rights.

It was my youth and inner strength that gave me the confidence to take this stance.

As a result of all the publicity, the matron of Royal Adelaide Hospital admitted me to continue my nursing training and I graduated as a charge nurse and stayed another 10 years.

In this period of my life, I realised that there were principles worth fighting for and that it was worth the energy to put up a good fight, if necessary, both for me as an individual and for all people disadvantaged by the attitudes of others.

Since then, I have worked for my people as a nurse and as an administrator. I have worked with many Aboriginal organisations and have been an adviser to both Commonwealth and State governments.

(continued)

Like other members of my race, I have experienced discrimination and frustration. I have developed different ways of coping.

I think I've always had a fairly positive attitude and the only times I've ever felt really angry is when I think about what happened to my mother.

I try to confront difficult situations with logic and humour.

As other people in leadership roles acknowledge, it is often lonely at the top. It seems people get the idea that you're 'untouchable', 'out-of-reach' or not a totally real person.

For me, the support of my own people has always given me strength. It is very important to me that people know they can contact me and that I am still a 'real person'.

My role as Chairperson of the Aboriginal and Torres Strait Islander Commission (ATSIC) has been the most important I've yet taken on. There has been a lot of criticism of ATSIC, maybe some that is valid. However, I see it as the best opportunity that has been presented to Aboriginal and Torres Strait Islander peoples in my lifetime to have a say in our destinies.

As a member of the Council for Aboriginal Reconciliation, I am working for a united and just Australia which values our heritage and recognises what we have contributed to this nation, and what we can and do contribute.

Reconciliation is for the benefit of all Australians, therefore it needs to be undertaken by both indigenous Australians and the wider community. An Australia that really appreciates Aboriginal and Torres Strait Islander cultures, and an Australia that could work together, would be a lovely place to live.

- Analyse all of the material above and list the main points made by the different people, both past and present, who are expressing a view on the issue. Produce a 500-word piece of writing expressing your understanding of the issue outlined in the material and explaining your view on Aboriginal reconciliation.

The approaches suggested below might help you find a way to write your response:
- You are an Aboriginal elder of a tribe today.
- You are Governor Phillip (as mentioned in 'Clashes between Whites and Aborigines').
- You are a newly arrived migrant with no understanding of Aboriginal history or culture.
- You are writing an article on the main features of reconciliation for your school newspaper.
- You are Lily's daughter. You are writing a letter to your mother.
- Your street has been invaded by a race from outer space. Your current way of life is prohibited and you are treated as a barbarian.

22 Understanding disability

Oh, there were some leaned on a stick
And some on stretchers lay,
But few walked on their own two feet
In the early green of day

David Campbell, Men in Green

Attitudes towards people with a disability are now considerably more enlightened than they were even 30 or 40 years ago. In the past, people with a disability could find themselves isolated and alone, or even locked away in an institution, particularly if they had no protective family or financial support.

Awareness has now become part of our thinking and attitudes have changed to a large degree. Today we are more conscious of the needs of people with disabilities. Buildings are equipped with special facilities, such as ramps for wheelchair access, and it is now possible to buy a car designed to allow easy access for a wheelchair and provide comfort for the person concerned. In many schools, support is available for students with a range of disabilities and teachers participate in training to understand such areas as partial blindness.

While these changes are occurring, there remain people within society who have little, if any, understanding of the nature of disability. For some, these attitudes come from a lack of knowledge and no comprehension of the frustrations and difficulties experienced by people with a disability. For others, these attitudes are deliberate and are adhered to with commitment. The issue is one of understanding the nature of difference.

Time to think

1 Read through each article below and make notes using the following suggestions as a guide. It might help to form discussion groups and work through the material together.
   - Skim read each article to gain a first impression of the subject.
   - Look at the titles of the articles. What comment can you make about the language? Why do you think particular words were chosen?
   - Reread each article carefully and note the main contention.
   - Write down any key words that suggest a particular tone and explain what is the tone of each article.
   - List any methods of persuasion or appeals to emotions, and so on, that the writer has used in each article (see Chapter 16).
   - Select one article and list the topic sentences of each paragraph.
   - Can you identify particular attitudes?
   - Where a photograph accompanies an article, describe your reaction to the photograph. Does it add to the article? Explain your response.
   - What knowledge have you gained from the articles?
   - State your attitude to the information presented in each.

The article below, 'Being a Mother Never Felt so Good' is by John Lahey (*Age*, 7 May 1994).

Being a mother never felt so good

Damien Kelly, born in Melbourne last November to parents who are totally blind, has become the sort of irresistible baby you feel like picking up and dancing with. Dum-dum-da-dum. Around the kitchen we go! You feel like blowing bubbles in his neck. He laughs when you do that.

He laughs or smiles at almost everything. Life is a marvellous joke. Anyone who thought that two blind people could not look after a baby is mad. His lively little eyes and his eager little fingers dart everywhere. He is sighted, for there was no reason that he should have been born blind. When his finger nails get long, his mother, Katrina, 26, bites them back to size.

I think I know what Mrs Kelly will do tomorrow on her first Mother's Day as a mother. She will hand Damien to her husband, Jamie, 27, a receptionist, and go back to bed. This has become the family's pattern at the weekends. Jamie Kelly takes over everything. Like every new mother, Mrs Kelly needs sleep, and the weekends are the time she has claimed to indulge herself. 'Nothing can deter me from sleep,' she said yesterday.

Many mothers would look longingly at Damien (six months old next Monday) for his ability to sleep through the night. He goes off at 8 pm, and doesn't wake until 6.30. He also has a nap in the morning and another in the afternoon. He has begun to eat solid food, and loves mashed vegetables.

Three days a week, he now goes to a creche, where the other children look forward to him because his mother's guide dog, Zoe, walks in with them.

They took Zoe with them to Brisbane in a plane recently to see Mrs Kelly's parents. 'It was a big effort taking the baby, Zoe and me,' Mrs Kelly said. 'Zoe was terrified on the plane. She kept trying to

Bath time: Damien Kelly and his mother Katrina share a moment of good, clean fun at home... but on Mother's Day she will be catching up on some much-needed sleep.

look out or get out the window, and Damien kept laughing.'

A second guide dog in the house is Windsor, who belongs to Jamie Kelly and goes with him to work at the talking-book library in South Yarra. These two dogs will not know what hit them when Damien becomes mobile. He can't wait to get his hands on them.

Mrs Kelly, a psychology graduate, is on maternity leave as a counsellor with the Commonwealth Rehabilitation Service.

(continued)

She has applied to resume work part-time on the three days a week when Damien is at the creche. Being alone so much in the house, she says, is tiring. 'It's the worst thing.' Too right it is, say a million women's voices.

Mrs Kelly isn't sure if she would like another baby. She begins by saying: 'I would like to have a second baby.' Then she says: 'Maybe.' Then: 'But I don't know. People say, "Oh, you forget the birth", but I don't see that you can.' Damien was born by caesarean section.

He had his triple-antigen injection recently and got the sniffles. His parents were able to take his temperature with their new thermometer sent to them by a friend in the United States. It is a talking thermometer. It doesn't merely register a temperature, it announces it.

Damien's nursery is a lovely, airy, colourful room, where mobiles hang, soft toys sit on shelves and a big floppy clown sprawls in the cot. Damien will realise one day how lucky he was to be born into a family which signposts every turning with love.

The advertisement below comes from the Commonwealth Rehabilitation Service.

The article below, 'Yes, Now I can Jump Waves Too' is by Caroline Overington (*Age*, 30 April 1994).

Yes, now I can jump waves too

The office of Bill Contoyannis is littered with body parts. He keeps his scissors in a hollow, rubber foot, his key ring is threaded with swatches of fake skin, varying in colour from pink to chocolate brown. Under his desk is a paisley-patterned plastic thigh: 'Some patients want something pretty. There is a whole range of hot pink, plastic legs walking around out there.'

And thanks to Mr Contoyannis and the staff at Monash University's Rehab-Tech, amputee Justin Lievesley, 21, has become the fourth best disabled water skier in the world only four years after losing both his legs.

Also walking – or, rather, bouncing – around out there is John Eden and his amazing J-shaped discus leg. It, and the pink and paisley legs, were designed by Mr Contoyannis, the manager of RehabTech, and his colleagues who create radically different arms, legs, elbows and knees for amputees who want to play sport but are frustrated by old fashioned limbs.

After Mr Lievesley, of Mount Evelyn, lost his legs when he fell asleep on a railway track, he decided to take up water skiing.

'Justin was certainly worse off than John, in terms of his injury slowing him down,' Mr Contoyannis said.

'He was a sporty sort of guy and wanted to try waterskiing.' Trouble was, he was so much better than the paraplegics because he had muscles in his lower body and thighs. We wanted him to harness that power.'

To aid Mr Lievesley, RehabTech attached a bucket seat to a surfboard-shaped ski. He shifts his weight from one side of the bucket to the other, tilting the ski to increase speed.

Justin Lievesley prepares for another session on the water as a friend, Alan Kempster, looks on. Since losing both legs in an accident four years ago, Justin has worked tirelessly at his sport so that he is now considered to be the fourth best disabled water skier in the world.

'There was no similar device anywhere in the world. We researched in Britain and the United States to find something suitable for him but there was nothing,' Mr Contoyannis said.

'Mr Lievesley said the tight bucket enabled him to use muscles in his thighs and buttocks: 'I'm made up with it,' he said.

One of the team's most successful projects was the development of Mr Eden's leg, which replaced one lost in a motorcycle accident. Surgeons had originally

(continued)

amputated his leg below the knee but after the operation he took to the rugby field and mangled the stump: 'I destroyed it,' he said cheerfully. 'They said they could save the knee but I'd never play sport again so I said: "Get rid of the knee",' Mr Eden now has only a short thigh.

'After the second operation, I took up discus but it was so boring. Amputees are supposed to stand there, then throw the discus. That's okay for the big guys but I was getting nowhere. I needed to be able to spin around, like they do in the Olympics,' he said.

Mr Eden came to the attention of RehabTech via the Australian Institute of Sport, which telephoned to say they had a miserable athlete: 'He was spinning on his artificial leg, cracking it and complaining,' Mr Contoyannis said.

The unit designed the FJ Leg – it is named after Mr Eden's first car – to operate as a giant spring, tossing him from one side of the discus circle to the other. He wore the leg to the Barcelona Paralympics and won silver.

RehabTech has also developed a titanium leg for a runner in Tasmania born with one shorter than the other, a gap which grew as he did. The new leg is strong enough to withstand kilometres of pounding punishment.

A one-armed patient from Melbourne was provided with a long claw for fishing. He was able to throw in a line, even get a bite, but could not bring in the catch. The extendable arm provides greater leverage.

The aim of RehabTech, Mr Contoyannis said, was to tackle any problem an athlete may have: 'If you blew your hands off and wanted to play golf, we would try to find a way to help you. More often, though, people who blow their hands off want to go mountain climbing: playing golf would be an easy assignment.'

He said Mr Eden's was a success story: 'Imagine you are a young guy; you've just had a leg blown off or torn off in an accident. You might not be able to go back to your old job – suddenly you have all this extra time on your hands; perhaps you even become an invalid pensioner. The psychological impact is enormous: you can start to feel like a hopeless cripple.'

'Sport can be a way out of the downward spiral. Eden can do anything. I can throw a discus about 15 metres with two good legs. He can throw it 40 metres bouncing around on one.'

RehabTech grew out of a Department of Veterans Affairs program to supply wooden legs and stump covers to returned servicemen. Before 1973, other amputees were treated in hospitals or managed without. The Whitlam Government decided there should be an artificial limbs unit for all people and handed the job to Veterans Affairs, since they were experts at the time.

Mr Contoyannis said the system worked until RehabTech staff began experimenting with highly scientific, specialised equipment like the FJ Leg. The unit was recently taken over by Monash University and moves to the Caulfield General Medical Centre next month.

The article below, 'Good Mates Don't Even Need to Talk to Each Other' is by John Lahey (*Age*, 10 May 1994).

Good mates don't even need to talk to each other

You could close your eyes and block your ears and stay that way for a month, but you still could not imagine what goes on in the mind of Pat Williams, 66, who is

(continued)

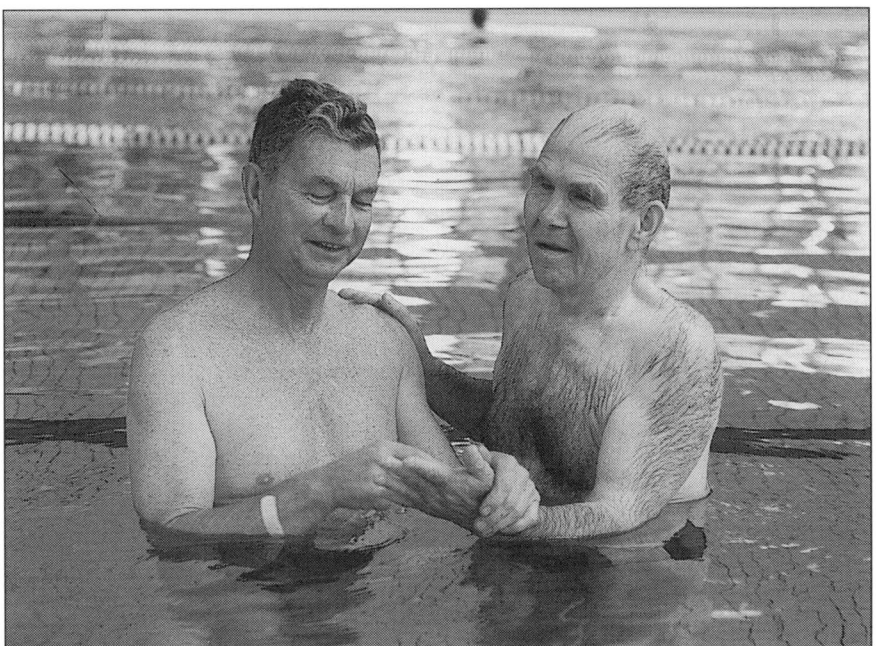

Mr Bill Wiles (left) spells out a message on the hand of Mr Pat Williams during one of their weekly visits to Nunawading swimming pool.

blind and profoundly deaf. He hears and sees nothing. Nor can he talk.

But he has a bonzer mate. For 14 years, Bill Wiles, 70, of Glen Waverley, has been taking Mr Williams once a week to a swimming pool, and he will continue to take him, he says, for as long as Mr Williams wants him to. 'I get as much out of it as he does, I think,' Mr Wiles says.

This is an unusual mateship. Most mates talk to each other easily. These two are limited. When Mr Wiles wants to tell Mr Williams something, he must take his hand and use it as a slate on which he spells out each word with his fingers. It is a slow method, devoid of any short cuts such as pointing or making a visual image, in the way that most deaf people know. There is no point in making a visual image to a blind man.

Mr Williams, however, does not have these constraints, for he is communicating with somebody sighted. He can point, perform mime and make gestures all he likes. Not all of this is clear to Mr Wiles, who says: 'This process makes small talk very difficult. Mainly our discussions are about things we need to know. I do not find it unduly difficult. The main problem is that I only use it once a week.'

The two met when Mr Wiles answered an advertisement in 1980 for volunteers to help look after the deaf. When he found himself with Mr Williams, who wanted to visit a pool once a week, neither could communicate with the other. Mr Wiles had to learn the special language they now use.

They have not entered each other's lives in any other way. Their contact is limited to weekly meetings of one hour at the Nunawading pool. Mr Wiles, a retired engineer, picks Mr Williams up at the home for deaf, Lakeside Lodge, in Blackburn, has a swim and a drink with him, and takes him home.

And yet Mr Wiles says he feels close to Mr Williams, and agrees readily that he regards him as a mate. He is not always sure what Mr Williams feels, 'but he is intelligent', he says. 'When we have a drink after our swim, he wants to know what the people around him are doing. He has obviously never been taught to speak, but he often tries to do so.'

'I admire him. I remember when he had pneumonia, and the doctor said he would have to stop smoking or he

(continued)

wouldn't last long. Pat used to roll his own, and you can imagine the tremendous pleasure it must have given a man who could neither see nor hear. Pat stopped smoking on the spot.'

'Diabetes was diagnosed once. One of the main things we talk about is food. Pat loved cakes and that sort of thing, but he gave them up. One thing about Pat is that he accepts these situations.'

When Mr Williams was recovering from angina, Mr Wiles did not take him to the pool. Instead they visited shopping centres all around Blackburn. Shopping centres usually display goods which can be felt. Mr Wiles says that Mr Williams can feel noise and weather. He has excellent craft skills, and has taken first prizes in cane work at the Royal Melbourne Show.

According to Dawn Williams, manager of Lakeside Lodge, Mr Williams apparently went deaf in his childhood, and went blind a few years later. She agrees that Mr Williams is very intelligent. 'He has limited speech. I can clearly understand some of what he is saying,' she says. The Victorian Deaf Society is among institutions making a special appeal this week for voluteer helpers.

In the pool, Mr Wiles constantly circles Mr Williams, who likes touching the bottom. He also likes playing ball. 'It is difficult to know if he can swim,' Mr Wiles says. 'We haven't been able to teach him to breathe properly.'

2 Watch the film *My Left Foot*, starring Daniel Day-Lewis, which is available on video. It is the story of Christy Brown and his struggle against cerebral palsy.

View the film without taking notes, but keep in mind the impact on a family when one of its members is disabled. In particular, consider the number of children in the family and the conditions in which they live.
- Imagine you are Christy Brown. Describe how you feel towards your family, in particular your mother.

3 Choose one of the following as the basis for an informative or persuasive essay of 500 to 600 words.
- Explain, using the information available to you and any other material, how today's society treats people with a disability.
- People with a disability have the same rights as everybody else.

4 In groups of five or six write and perform a short play showing one or more aspects of the issue of disability in society today.

5 Choose one of the above articles on disability and write a poem exploring the issues raised in the article.

Appendix 1
The Language of Thinking

This section includes definitions of important terms used in critical and creative thinking.

affirmative   arguing for a particular point of view; state as fact
analogy   a comparison made showing the similarities between two different things as a means of explaining an idea.
analyse   examine minutely the parts of an argument
argument   reason advanced for or against an aspect of an issue
attitude   settled opinion and behaviour
authority   conclusive opinion or statement; a person who has expert knowledge in a given field
bias   predisposition; prejudice; influence
brainstorm   spontaneous discussion in search of new ideas
cause   an action that produces an effect on someone or something
comparison   observation of the similarities between two things
contention   point of view in an argument
debate   engage in formal argument or discussion
effect   a result or consequence produced by the action of someone or something
evidence   facts available as proof
expert   a person having special skill or knowledge in a particular area
fact   something that has been established as true
generalisation   a general statement based on too few instances
issue   a subject on which there exists more than one point of view
lateral thinking   seeking to solve problems by means other than conventional logic
logic   the science of reasoning
modify   to qualify or change the strength of a viewpoint
negative   against a particular point of view
objective   impartial; without bias or prejudice
opinion   a point of view about something
persuade   an attempt to influence another's point of view
positive   in favour of a particular point of view
prejudice   prior judgement about a group or an issue
qualify   to change or modify the strength of a viewpoint
rational   a logical or reasoned approach
rationalisation   finding reasons to justify a point of view
subjective   based on feelings and emotions
value judgement   a statement that someone or something is good or bad

Bibliography

Burton-Taylor, Jane, 'Understanding Children', *Simply Living*, March 1994.

Cooke, Giselle, 'The Medical Outcome: Thirty Years of Cannibis Use', *Simply Living*, March 1994.

De Bono, Edward, *Six Thinking Hats*, Pelican Books, London, 1987.

——, *Teach Your Child to Think*, Penguin, Harmondsworth, 1993.

Elder, Bruce, *Blood on the Wattle*, National Book Distributors, Sydney, 1988.

Eysneck, H.J., *Know Your Own IQ*, Penguin, Harmondsworth, 1962.

Humana, Charles, *World Human Rights Guide*, Oxford University Press, New York, 1992.

Maclagan, David, *Creation Myths: Man's Introduction to the World*, Thames & Hudson, London, 1977.

Mee, Arthur (ed.), *The Children's Encyclopedia*, vols 1 & 2, Educational Book Company, London.

Roberts, Ainslie and Mountford, Charles, *The Dreamtime Book: Australian Aboriginal Myths*, Rigby, Melbourne, 1976.

West, A.S., *The Revised English Grammar*, University Press, Cambridge, 1923.

Further Reading

Critical and Creative Thinking

De Bono, Edward, *I Am Right, You Are Wrong*, Penguin, London, 1991.
——, *Six Action Shoes*, Fontana, London, 1992.
——, *Teaching Thinking*, Penguin, London, 1976.

Human Rights

Allende, Isabel, *Of Love and Shadows*, Black Swan, London, 1993.
Bitton Jackson, Livia E., *Elli Coming of Age in the Holocaust*, Harper Collins, London, 1980.
Cassidy, Sheila, *Audacity to Believe*, Collins Dove, Melbourne, 1977.
Wiesel, Elie, *Night*, Penguin, London, 1960.

Disability

Connaughton, Shane and Sheridan, Jim, *My Left Foot*, produced by Noel Pearson, directed by Jim Sheridan, A Granada Film, Sovereign Pictures, 1989.
Dodd, Bill, *Broken Dreams*, University of Queensland Press, St Lucia, 1992.
Keller, Helen, *The Story of My Life*, Dell Publishing, New York, 1961.
Marshall, Alan, *I Can Jump Puddles*, Cheshire, Melbourne, 1965.
Moorhouse, Jocelyn, *Proof*, produced by Lynda House, in association with the Australian Film Commission and Film Victoria, House and Moorhouse Films (Australia) Pty Ltd, 1991.
Shakespeare, Rosemary, *The Psychology of Handicap*, Methuen, London, 1975.

Aborigines

Horton (ed.), *The Aboriginal Encyclopaedia of Australia*, 2 vols, Aboriginal Studies Press for the Australian Institute of Aboriginal and Torres Strait Islander Studies, Canberra, 1994.
Keneally, Thomas, *Flying Hero Class*, Hodder & Stoughton, 1991.
Langton, M. and Peterson, N. (eds), *Aborigines, Land and Land Rights*, Australian Institute of Aboriginal Studies, Canberra, 1983.
Morgan, Sally, *My Place*, Fremantle Arts Centre Press, 1987.
Walking Together, a kit compiled by the Council for Aboriginal Reconciliation, Canberra, 1994.
Weller, Archie, *The Day of the Dog*, Allen & Unwin, Sydney, 1981.

Acknowledgments

The author thanks colleagues, including Jackie Holston, Nola Schlegel, Robin Timmins and Barry Upton, for their advice and support; Wendy Anderson and Jo McMillan of Oxford University Press for their guidance; the students who have allowed their work to be published; and Simon Gardiner from Music-Inn, Ivanhoe, for his assistance in locating the lyrics of 'Tar and Cement'.

Source acknowledgments
The author and publishers are grateful to copyright holders for permission to reproduce copyright material:

Age for the photographs on pp. 157, 159, 161; AGPS for the advertisement for 'Commonwealth Rehabilitation Service' on p. 158, Commonwealth of Australia Copyright reproduced with permission; Australian Associated Press for the photograph on p. 144; Pamela Bone for 'Words and excuses fail when children are innocent victims', from *Age*, 25 July 1994; Jamie Brown for 'Fighting Fires With Rhetoric', from *Simply Living*, March 1994; Council for Aboriginal Reconciliation for 'The Key Issues of Reconciliation', reproduced with permission from Council for Aboriginal Reconciliation's *Sharing Our Future* supplement as appeared in *Weekend Australian*, 13–14 August 1994 and for 'Lily's Daughter: A Life of Hope' by Lois O'Donoghue, reproduced with permission from Council for Aboriginal Reconciliation's *Walking Together: Building Better Relationships between All Australians*; Crash Test Dummies, *Mmm Mmm Mmm*, Brad Roberts, Polygram Music, BMG Music, Canada Inc. 1993; EMI for *Tar and Cement*, Verdelle Smith (Vance/Pockriss/Beretta/Del Prete/Calentano); John Fahey for 'Being a mother never felt so good', from *Age*, 7 May 1994 and 'Good mates don't even need to talk to each other', from *Age*, 10 May 1994; Martin Flanagan for 'Never Give Up, Says An Angel Named Henry', from *Age*, 7 June 1994; Gaia Books, London for 'Forests of the future' from *The Gaia Atlas of Planet Management* by Norman Myers; Enrica Longo for 'Parents not buying ads for children' by Enrica Longo, from *Age*, 6 April 1994; Steve Malcolm for 'The Greenhouse Effect on Life on Earth' by Steve Malcolm, from *Age*, 7 June 1994; Microsoft Corporation for 'What you really want from a computer'; Sue Neales for 'Gender Roles still entrenched' by Sue Neales, senior journalist with *Age* newspaper, Melbourne, from *Age*, 16 December 1993; Auspac Media for 'Earthweek: Diary of A Planet', Copyright 1994 CHRONICLE FEATURES; Newsday for 'Baby Amina joins Rwanda's Darwinian tussle' by Dele Olojede, from *Age*, 25 July 1994; Nintendo for 'Nintendo and Epilepsy—The Links Explored', from *Nintendo Magazine System*, May 1993; Caroline Overington for 'Yes, now I can jump waves too', from *Age*, 30 April 1994; Bruce Petty/*Age* for the cartoon on p. 89; Henry Reynolds for 'Invasion versus settlement debate wears on', from *Weekend Australian*, 13–14 August 1994; *Scientific American*, Time Life Picture Library and N.A.S.A. for 'Digital Photomontage', from *Scientific American*, February 1994; Spooner for the cartoons on pp. 87, 88; Talking Heads (Byrne, Frantz, Harrison), *Nothing But Flowers*, Indec Music Inc./Bleu Disque Music Co. Inc. (ASCAP).

Disclaimer
Every effort has been made to trace the original source material contained in this book. Where the attempt has been unsuccessful, the publishers would be pleased to hear from copyright holders to rectify any omissions.

Index

Aborigines
   reconciliation 147–54
advertisements 104–7
alliteration 109
analogies 77–81
   how they work 78
   why they are used 79–80
appeal, methods of 104–5
argument 64
   counter 64
   definitions of 64
   supporting an 64, 66
argumentative essays 64–5
   body 64
   building 64
   conclusion 65, 67
   creating style in 66
   drafting 68–74
   effective writing in 66
   introduction 64, 67
   planning 67
   rebuttal 64
   student writing 68–73
   writing effectively 66
attitudes, changing 94
audience 23–6, 57
   recognising 25

'Baby Amina joins Rwanda's Darwinian tussle' 144–5
'Being a mother never felt so good' 157–8
bias 18
body paragraphs 36–7
brainstorming 82–5

caption 88
cartoons
   analysing 88
   responding to 89
   visual message in 87

cause 46–54
   establishing 48
conclusion 37–8
contention 29, 64
   statements of 31
creative thinking 99–102

debates
   adjudicator 115
   affirmative team 114
   chairperson 115
   first speaker 114
   language in 117
   manner 116
   matter 115–16
   method 117
   negative team 114
   objective in 114
   second speaker 114
   third speaker 115
   timekeeper's role 115
de Bono, Edward 100, 129
   Six Thinking Hats 100
dialogue 88
'Digital Photomontage' 43–4
disability 156
drafting 68–74

'Earthweek: Diary of a Planet' 49
effect 46–54
The Emerald Forest 121–6
emotions, in advertising 104–5
evaluation, in informative writing 57
evidence 9, 14, 19
   supporting 34, 64
expert information 109

facts 9–10, 12
   identifying 12
   questioning 9

film
   audience and purpose in 121, 124
   conflicts, issues, points of view in 124
   first impressions in 122
   information, facts, details in 122
   responding to 122–6
   solving problems for the future in 126
   viewing and comprehension in 123
'Fighting Fires With Rhetoric' 110–12
'Forests of the future' 19–21

'Gender roles still entrenched' 12
generalisations 14–22
   bias in 18
   complex 18
   evidence in 19
   identifying 15–16
   language of 16–17
   simple 17–18
   value judgements in 18
'Good mates don't even need to talk to each other' 160–2
'The Greenhouse Effect on Life on Earth' 50

idea, development of 64
images, visual 88
inform, ways to 59
informative writing 55–62
   audience in 57
   evaluation in 57
   purpose in 57
introduction 34–6

'Invasion versus settlement debate wears on' 148–51
issue 31, 64

labels 88
language
  in generalisations 16
  modifying 16
  objective 64
  of influence 103, 109–12
  qualifying 16
  subjective 64
'Life, Death and the News' 143
'Lily's Daughter: A Life of Hope' 152–4
linking words 38–9

methods of persuasion 104
'MMM MMM MMM MMM' (Crash Test Dummies) 47
My Left Foot 162

'Never Give Up, Says An Angel Named Henry' 51–2
'Nintendo and Epilepsy— The Links Explored' 58–9
nostalgia 110
'(Nothing but) Flowers' (Talking Heads) 95–7
Night (Elie Wiesel) 142

opinion 9–12,
  expressing 11
  identifying 12
  supporting 9

paragraphs
  body 36–7
  conclusion 37–8
  definition of 34
  introduction 34–6
  persuasive 33–7
  structuring 36
'Parents not buying ads for children' 65–6
persuasive devices
  alliteration 109
  expert information 109
  nostalgia 110
  paragraphs 33–7
  repetition 109
  rhetorical question 109
  sadness 110
  statistics 109–10
  sympathy 110
  tone 110
persuasive writing 34
photographs 89–92
planning 67
  creative 82–5
point of view 64
problem solving 128–31
  for the future 126
purpose 23–6, 57
  recognising 25

rebuttal 64

repetition 109
rhetorical question 109

sadness 110
Select Documents in Australian History (Manning Clark) 147–8
signs 88
slogans 105, 108
statistics 109–10
summary 40–5
  definition of 41
  who uses them 41
symbols 88
sympathy 110

'Tar and Cement' (Verdelle Smith) 94–5
tone 110
topic sentences 30, 64
  in paragraphs 36
transition words 38

unbiased 56
Universal Declaration of Human Rights 136–9

value judgements 18
viewpoint 27–32
  expressing 31
  finding a 28
'Words and excuses fail when children are innocent victims' 140–1

'Yes, now I can jump waves too' 159–60